Making It
In Washington

An Essential Guide for Political Appointees

by

Dave Oliver, Jr.

Cover
by
Patti Scully-Lane

TRAFFORD

National Library of Canada Cataloguing in Publication

Oliver, Dave, 1941-
   Leadership and management in Washington / Dave Oliver Jr.
ISBN 1-55395-172-7
   I. Title.

JK692.O45 2002   351.73   C2002-904640-8

TRAFFORD

This book was published *on-demand* in cooperation with Trafford Publishing.
On-demand publishing is a unique process and service of making a book available
for retail sale to the public taking advantage of on-demand manufacturing and
Internet marketing.**On-demand publishing** includes promotions, retail sales,
manufacturing, order fulfilment, accounting and collecting royalties on behalf
of the author.

Suite 6E, 2333 Government St., Victoria, B.C. V8T 4P4, CANADA
Phone   250-383-6864   Toll-free   1-888-232-4444
Fax   250-383-6804   E-mail   sales@trafford.com
Website   www.trafford.com
TRAFFORD PUBLISHING IS A DIVISION OF TRAFFORD HOLDINGS LTD.
Trafford Catalogue #02-0886   www.trafford.com/robots/02-0886.html

10   9   8   7   6   5   4   3

I would like to thank several people who gave a great deal of their personal time in assisting me with ideas and context — Liz Bailey, Jim Bailey, Mike Bayer, Hans Binnedijk, Irv Blickstein, Jay Davis, Jim Durso, Delores Etter, Jack Gansler, Mary Gropp, Bill Houley, Ellie Johnson, Dave McGiffert, Dick Moose, Terry Myers, Dorothy Oliver, Tim Oliver, Bill Reinsch, Tom Ricks, Lynn Selfridge, Chuck Sieber, Maureen Steiner, Nancy Spruill, Steve Spruill, Joe Trento, Mitzi Wertheim, Leslie and Mike Zimring. I needed and appreciated all of your help.

The book is dedicated to my best friend
Linda Bithell Oliver
Originally of Blackfoot, Idaho.
An attorney and career government civil servant.

Table of Contents

LEADERSHIP AND MANAGEMENT IN WASHINGTON

Unlike any other nation in the world, in the United States we fill nearly every senior supervisory job in our Government with political appointees. These men and women alight for awhile in Washington, only to depart again with each change of the White House, or more frequently, as their careers and family call them home.

There is no standard profile of a political appointee; some have been financial contributors, others were volunteers in the national campaign, individuals with special knowledge and talents, or staff personnel from Congress. They are all very bright, educated and motivated. On the other hand, individuals selected may have very limited experience in the practice of leadership or in the day-to-day management of the large staffs they inherit.

The fact that these exceptional Americans do as well as they do is both a credit to themselves as well as to the people and process that nominates and appoints each. However, there is *no training* and *no time* for them to prepare. As a result, political appointees often start out less effective than they might be, and valuable time is lost in moving the President's agenda along. With some help, they, and the Administration, can have more impact.

This book is a guide to those who would serve, to those who support them, and to students of both leadership and management. It is a "how to," with case studies of successes, as well as failures, in our Capitol Region.

The principles herein apply to the relationships all Departments and Agencies in the Executive Branch of our Government have with each other, the White House, the Congress, career civil servants and representatives of other governments. In addition, especially in the Pentagon, the military are also players, which adds additional complexity to the political appointees' leadership and management responsibilities.

Whichever job the political appointee is given the opportunity to fill, he or she is an essential member of the Team which America holds responsible for keeping the torch of freedom, as well as the many candles of democracy, burning bright for all the world to see.

Chapter One

GETTING CONFIRMED

The President has asked you to help him run the Government! Congratulations! In all likelihood, you are about to embark on the highlight of your life. No matter what responsibility you will hold, it will make your previous professional experiences pale in comparison. It will be an episode in your life which you will always remember. Your responsibilities will drain you emotionally and tax you physically. After it is over, the experience will be the touchstone by which you measure your contribution to America.

This book is to help you become effective as soon as possible, so that you can carry out the President's programs, improve your Department or Agency, make the world a better and safer place, and sleep more easily when the job is done.

If you are one of the several hundred Presidential Appointees who require Senate confirmation, the first step is getting you confirmed. If you are one of the other thousands of people who have been selected to have important political jobs that do not require confirmation, the confirmation process is still of interest, because you will be helping fellow political appointees achieve confirmation, and may, later in the Administration, yourself be nominated to a Senate-confirmed job. If the reader is a civil servant, pay attention, since, depending on your role in your Bureau, you may have to do much of the work!

After the President announces his "intent to nominate," there are six formal parts to the confirmation process: preparation, filling out the forms, calls on the Senators and their key staff members, the Committee hearing, the vote by the Congress and the subsequent approval by the President. There is also an informal aspect. How well you do in this unofficial facet is often a reflection of your people skills (good ones will prove invaluable in Washington). Let me give you a personal example of how, at one step, I faltered and recovered.

My nomination had stalled for four months in the Senate for no specific reason, and the Administration was trying hard, but fruitlessly, to get me aboard. I believed I could identify the Senator who was the stumbling block — he had sensed during my interview that I was not in agreement on one of his key issues. I thought I had skated over the thin ice portion of our discussion, but it is the rare Capitol Hill denizen who is not very, very perceptive. The Senator had no information to actively oppose me on my record, but he was no friend of the Administration, and maybe I hadn't pirouetted quite as nicely as I remembered.

I reflected. Who could convince the Senator to silently give way? And then I recalled a friend who is the godson of a (very influential) second Senator. A few phone calls, some candid explanations, and a couple of days later I am having breakfast with the godson.

The interview most critical to my confirmation thus took place over bagels. We talked for a couple of hours about old friends, and common battles, and the importance of local politics upon even national figures. The godson "suggested" that I might want to visit several local places in key states so I fully understood how important a few issues were to people. One of the places he mentioned was a restaurant a thousand miles away.

"Maybe you could meet a couple of the Senator's old friends

tomorrow night at Brett Favre's bar on the bayou at Ocean Grove?"
"Sure." (Well, what would you have said? He was offering me
a second chance to recover my initial interview fumble. Even if it
turned out to be a snipe hunt, I wanted the nomination. I can do
snipe hunts. I was a Boy Scout.)

The next evening, I found a small place Brett had reportedly
been seen walking by once or twice in the off-season. Inside, I
introduced myself to several men and women who had been having a weekly dinner at the same table for longer than any of them
could remember. We spent the evening discussing politics, foot-
ball, shrimp po'boys, America's role in the world, and how my
wife and I had enjoyed the area when we lived here several years
ago. The subject of my nomination never came up. We just talked,
while the moisture beaded and rolled down the pitchers and glasses,
forming neat rings on the oilcloth. We talked until the entire table
was wet.

The Senate found me acceptable the next week.

You can not afford to stumble at any step. That caution behind
us, let's walk through the formal process.

First, let's consider that thick sheave of forms you have been
asked to fill out. All appointments are the President's. They do not
"belong" to your Secretary or other non-elected individuals, although, in practice, each Administration decides how much they
will "negotiate" these appointments with its Cabinet Secretaries.

No matter how you came to the attention of the President and
the team which is charged with filling the jobs in an Administration, once nominated, you become a direct reflection upon the President's judgment, whether you are his brother, or someone he would
not recognize if he bumped into you coming out of the Lincoln
bathroom. The President is the one elected.

He and his people, after all their hard work to get him elected,
are not going to be interested in any of your concerns about privacy. They are going to have to live with what you do after you are
confirmed. They are not interested in being embarrassed by something you may have done or said before you became their responsibility. The paperwork helps the President's staff learn more about

you. So, quit whining and fill out the voluminous forms. Before you were considered for nomination, you have already been checked out informally. Some staffers at the White House and in the Department have called your friends, and as many enemies as they could locate, to see if you have obvious unacceptable flaws. Once you passed that process, and the President decided on you, it is time to call in the FBI and do the whole process more completely. No President likes to be surprised. Any omission you might make in your answers to the White House, verbally, or in the paperwork, will be frowned upon if it comes up during your confirmation process. The error not only endangers your successful nomination, it also holds up everyone behind you, as staffers scramble to find out how this problem slipped by the process, and add another question or two to the forms.

The Senate will ask for many of the same answers, so keep a copy of everything.

By the way, unless you are independently very wealthy, after the President or his staff called you with the happy news, I hope you didn't quit your day job, sell your house, and move to Washington. You didn't, did you? Good! Several have, to their great regret (and fiscal loss). Not acting precipitously is a start toward demonstrating an acceptable political appointee IQ. (Most firms are more than willing to put up with your erratic pre-confirmation schedule.)

Either after, or sometimes simultaneously with, filling out the forms, it becomes time to prepare you for the "dialogue" with the Senate which is the essence of the confirmation process.

The staff you will inherit, and people assigned by your Department/Service/Agency congressional relations office, will help you prepare for the formal interviews. This help specifically includes assistance from the career civil servants. Don't underestimate the interest and support the "bureaucrats" will offer. They want you confirmed quickly. Without you, they are largely marking time, for you will be their voice and official entrée to the rest of the Department and Administration. You are going to empower their work!

The Staff will have a book, or books, about the programs for which you will be responsible, as well as information on Senators and their key issues. These preparatory books are often voluminous, because each of your staff-to-be wants to make sure you understand both the importance of their programs, as well as (naturally) the importance of each of them.

But before you start reading the books and talking to your staff, there are two rules you must remember, no matter how long the confirmation process may take:

Don't presume confirmation, and

Don't appear to be making decisions

Don't Presume Confirmation

Don't move into the office which will be yours (I know, you may have heard of someone who did so, and got away with it, but why seize the opportunity to screw up early?). Moving into "your" office can be seen by the Senate as presuming confirmation, which is the major no-no at this point in the process. In addition, you don't want to be seen by your staff-to-be as pompous, unwilling to participate in the process, and a general *prima donna*. In that vein, do not start using any of the other prerogatives which the office may bring with it — the driver, the parking space, the Executive Assistant, etc.

A special note about Defense. Some Senate committees allow nominees to come on board as paid consultants during the confirmation process, but not the Senate Armed Services Committee. At Defense you can only come to the office to be briefed on your future responsibilities.

During this confirmation process, <u>don't make decisions or offer public comments about issues on which you may be briefed or in meetings to which you may be invited.</u> Unless you are unusual, you do not yet know the politics of the issues, and, no matter how qualified, you have no standing in the Administration. You do not want to express an opinion which you may have to eat, along with a side dish of crow, when you better understand where your new boss stands on the issue. Finally, the Committee responsible for your Confirmation looks upon anything that smells like a decision as an action "presuming confirmation." Arlington Cemetery is the resting place not only for some great Americans, but also for the political bones of many outstanding appointees who were never confirmed as a result of statements, letters, or emails that the Committee construed as presuming confirmation. Usually a new President's first appointees (Secretary of State, Secretary of Defense, etc.) sail through confirmation without a lot of kowtowing. From the rest of us, the Hill demands respect.

Vigilance is the word of the day. If you have not been cautious, a good grovel can sometimes be a successful atonement. I never liked groveling, but to each their own.

It is also important to remember that you are not yet part of a "team." Once you are in, the "team" may well protect the "odd" (foolish) statement that crosses your lips. But you will find the career civil servants (and, in the case of Defense, the military) have a higher sense of loyalty to those who are on the team than to mere pretenders. During the nomination period you are particularly vulnerable.

An appointee who is not confirmed, as a result of a comment he/she may have made, is frequently viewed as a scalp on the belt of the press or the party not in power. A new Administration doesn't have much of a track record at this time, and the misstep, or per-ceived misstep, of a Presidential Appointee always gets reported far and wide, and is considered an early reflection, however accurate, on the President's and his Administration's judgment. Keep your lip buttoned!

No matter how well qualified you may be, no nomination is ever a "mortal lock," as the sportscasters say. Only an unknown has never done something that might make some Senator, Member of Congress or one of their constituents, upset. And unknowns do not become potential Presidential appointees. The Senate is willing to give the President his appointees – if they are qualified.

But different people and different interest groups might well have very diverse ideas about what "qualified" means. In addition, once confirmed, you are going to have a great deal of personal discretionary authority. And you are not going to be directly responsible to the voters. So the Senate considers each potential nominee carefully. Consideration takes time. I waited a long time from the moment the Armed Services Committee voted unanimously in favor of my approval before the Senate finally confirmed my appointment. Many have waited longer, or never been confirmed. Why?

Because it's a political process. Between the time you are nominated and the day the Senate confirms, you have a disproportionate value to anyone who opposes the President or even a "friend" who might happen to want something from the President or your Department/Agency. You would be surprised by the things that have been "traded" in order to get key Administration jobs manned and running. The initial asking price for a friend of mine was a billion dollar ship a particular Senator wanted added to the Defense budget request.

This was too high a price to pay for an Assistant Secretary! However, the Senator remained firm and the nomination gathered dust in the Hart Senate Office Building. Many calls were made, various postures were struck, and alternate deals were proposed, considered and discarded by one side or the other. Months passed. Senate recesses (during which no floor action, including confirmations, is taken) came and went with the Washington seasons. "Perhaps a smaller ship?" suggested the ship-Senator. No, still too much.

Finally, nearly a year later, the ship-Senator was looking for an additional few votes for one of his own proposals. The Defense Congressional Relations staff watched carefully as he searched. He looked a vote short. Finally, a second Senator suggested to one of our staff that he might be willing to swing his vote to the ship-Senator's side if only he were more comfortable with the security of systems for storing information in Defense.

"What is the problem," we asked? "We have the best safes made!"

"The safes are okay, but what about the filing cabinet locks? I believe in the importance of keeping all Defense information out of the hands of the wrong people. I have always worried that Defense buys filing cabinet locks overseas, not using the best ones available, which are manufactured right here in the USA." (Through fortuitous circumstance the only acceptable quality cabinet lock was manufactured in the second Senator's state.)

"In fact," the Senator continued, "I bet you wouldn't have had that problem at Los Alamos, if you only had better cabinet locks."

Well, the Los Alamos "problem" had nothing to do with Defense, and wasn't due to "inadequate" cabinet locks, but it also takes a humongous number of locks to come even close to the price of even a very small ship.

After due deliberation, and a review of how many new cabinet locks we were going to use over the next few years, Defense ordered some "good American" cabinet locks to hold the Canadian paper imprinted by Singaporean printers. The lock-Senator talked to the ship-Senator. Who knows what was said? The results were good. Eleven months after he was nominated (and a year after he had sold his house and moved to Washington from California!!!), my friend was confirmed.

It is all part of the process, but it is also serious business. Respect the process, keep in good touch with your real friends and continue to do the things that got you nominated in the first place. Recognize that, even if you are Mother Teresa's first cousin, it may take the best part of a year to negotiate the proper "considerations." Keep your day job and don't resign from the local PTA.

Let's return to the paperwork. Please do not permit the size of the preparation task to upset you. If you require Senate confirmation, remember your job carries more responsibility than that of the CEO of the largest corporation in the world. Of course there is a great deal to learn, and of course there will be an endless line of your staffers "to be" who want to give you interminable briefings. The fact that they are interested is terrific. It means they believe in the importance of their jobs. You would not want them to think anything else (in part, because you are going to find you don't have sufficient time to micromanage their performance).

This is your first chance to see which staff members can express their thoughts clearly and succinctly. This is also your first opportunity to judge which issue answers are, in your opinion, misguided, and will need further examination, either (but not usually) before the hearing or after confirmation. In addition, this is often your first exposure to the scope of your responsibilities. Read the issue papers as carefully as you are wont for information, ask questions about issues you feel are important, and prepare yourself as best you can in the time available. Until now, you probably have been unaware of some of the topics thrust into your hands. Don't worry. Unless you have been involved in government all your life, this is normal.

Remember, Administration appointees come and go, and Senators see this process every year. They will not expect the incoming appointee to have full command of each issue. That said, the Senate will still expect you to grasp the essence of the issues they and their staff have identified in the questions which they send you. Your staff will draft the answers and you should carefully edit them before submission. Remember, they are <u>your answers</u>, not the staff's.

It is not too soon to point out a key fact which will bear repeating – the hearing is, in part, to ensure you recognize the role of the Congress, and your responsibilities to answer their calls for testimony and information. They are looking for honest answers and your recognition that they have a right to be part of the process.

The hearing will also be the opportunity for the Senate or a specific member to <u>try</u> to get you on record as supporting a particular policy (which the President or Secretary may or may not support) of specific interest to a Senator or constituent. Before you put an answer in the record which you may later regret, realize you have a choice. You are not expected to have every answer at your fingertips. You are not in office, yet. You do not have to have a position, yet. You don't have to deliver an answer, yet. The benefit of the doubt always goes to the President's candidate (and you may well want to maintain "decision flexibility" for when you are in office).

On the other hand, you do not want to appear foolish (unfamiliar in general with a subject of common Congressional or public interest), or evasive. If you disagree with what a Senator obviously desires, and/or have not previously discussed this with the President or Secretary as to what either wants to say and when and how they want it said (which would be the situation in most instances), you should state, "Let me take that question for the record, Senator, and, if confirmed, I will get back to you." It is best to give this general answer early in the questioning, rather than later. There will inevitably be questions you are not prepared to answer. This is not a problem, for at this point in the process you are not expected to know your area of responsibility as well as you will (or as well as many Senator's think they do).

This is a confirmation, not testimony (which will be discussed later). This is a "pass-fail" test. You are not graded. An "A" isn't necessary, but just like high school, you have to pass to move on.

While you are preparing for the coming grilling, it is also time for you, along with your "minder" (the Department/Agency or Service staffer who normally deals with that committee), to make courtesy calls on the key Senators and staff members who are interested in your area of responsibility. The call is usually a pleasant experience. However, recognize it also as a tremendous occasion to build relationships.

However little or much time the Senator or staffer gives you, this is an important job interview. A misstep here might cost you "your" job (remember my fumble recovery trip to the bayou?), and will definitely make your next few years unnecessarily much more difficult.

Your objective for the call is to establish a personal relationship which emphasizes your integrity, your ability to listen, and your intent to do the most professional job possible. For those Senators and key staffers you do not know well, listen carefully to what they identify or imply may be their important issues. Discussion topics will not have been selected at random. Even if the Senator is not particularly interested in you, his or her staff will have provided several questions on issues about which they will ensure the Senator becomes concerned, even if he is not at the moment. There is information even in the silences. Don't waste this opportunity.

Also remember that your "minder" is going to be a key person in your success with the Congress. He or she is the daily contact with that committee and staff. The good ones know all the issues and hot buttons of the day and are trusted by the Congress.

This may be confusing for a while, but several Departments have two or more different organizations dealing with Congress. As you might expect, depending primarily on personalities, those several organizations may not communicate internally terribly well.

For example, the shop which has the label "Congressional Relations" deals with the Authorization committees and all Members of Congress who are not on the two Appropriations committees. Concurrently, the Comptroller's shop manages relations with the Senators and Representatives on the Appropriations (money) committees.

In Defense, each Military Service also has a Congressional Relations staff, as does each Bureau in Commerce, as well as the Commerce Department, etc. The same split of Congressional responsibilities exists in all Departments and Agencies. No matter how confusing the "Authorization" and "Appropriations" split may be to you, this is the way Congress wants it, so you will have to learn to be alert to the nuances.

By the way, whoever your minders are, they are inevitably going to discuss your performance with their peers in their shop, as well as submit a short note on your performance to the Secretary. You are making your first impressions with more than the Senate.

Welcome to the major leagues.

The fourth major step in the confirmation process is the actual hearing with your Department's Senate Committee. No matter how pro forma your intelligence may indicate the hearing will be, you need a "murder board," also known as a mock hearing. If one isn't scheduled, schedule one for yourself. Invite your minders from Congressional Relations (one of them has the responsibility to get you through), someone from the Comptrollers shop, and the most senior people in the Department who are available to attend.

Your goal is to receive tough questions, hopefully with a slant you haven't considered, and answer them, at the same pace, and in the same manner, as you will in the hearing room. Practice the way you intend to testify. Expect your board members to critically monitor, not only the answers, but also your style and body language, as the Senate members will be hearing, seeing and evaluating the whole.

Leadership Rules

Whatever else you may take away from this murder board, make sure it includes the following:

- The Staff responsible for Congressional relations know the Congress. Listen to them.
- If you cannot provide a clear and concise answer, don't attempt to construct one during the hearing. You can always take a question for the record (and subsequently get the entire Department to help you craft the proper answer).
- Remember you aren't confirmed until after the Senate hearing and the President's signature. Consequently, ensure you say words to the effect, "If confirmed, I will ..." (rather than, "I will....") often enough to keep the Committee comfortable. Don't presume confirmation.
- You want to be part of the Administration Team. Don't let false pride become an insurmountable obstacle.
- The Senate knows its role. (As a Defense example, Article I, Section 8 of the Constitution states that Congress shall have the power:
  "To raise and support Armies:
  To provide and maintain a Navy ....' etc.)
- Before you are sworn in, Congress wants to ensure you have a clear appreciation of their legal and historical role in Government.

Management Rules:

- Carefully observe the unwritten rules which accompany the nomination and confirmation process.
- You are being observed and judged from the first day of the process. Act accordingly.
- Confirmation is a "pass-fail" test. Save your home run swing for future testimony. You are going to get several at bats.

And remember the bottom line:

- Congress has final approval and the money — your Department/Agency needs both.

Chapter Two

ORGANIZING YOUR OFFICE

Well done! The Senate has concurred in the President's decision to nominate you. Just when you thought it was all over, you have discovered that, due to a little disagreement between the President and Congress back in the 1800s, your confirmed nomination now has to go back to the White House to see if the President still wants you after (your hearing testimony, and) the Senate vote.

And the President wants to personally sign your appointment in order to preserve that ancient Supreme Court decision. It normally takes four or more days for the documents to move and this process to be completed. As soon as the nondescript White House document arrives, it is time to take the oath of office. The great looking sheepskin certificate for your wall won't arrive for several months.

Swearing In

Enjoy the moment. Often, for more senior officials, the swearing-in is done twice. Once, to be official, so you can start work immediately, and a second time within a couple of weeks, to give adequate notice for friends and family to assemble and witness your proud moment. Frequently the official swearing-in is your first "public" appearance, so make sure your short speech (I would like to thank my dance teacher, my mother and all four of my stepfathers, etc.) are brief and appropriate.

It is your moment, but you are joining a new team, many of whom you may not yet know well, and all of whom are secretly wondering if you can do your new job. This is a moment to enjoy, and, like the Senate hearing, an opportunity to exercise some self-restraint. Those first impressions are lasting. I once saw a new appointee who had carefully written his remarks to include several obscure references to his academic field of expertise. That might have been okay, since no one usually remembers what was said at these things, but in this case, his new boss was also an expert in the same field and had introduced him using similar alliterations. When the new appointee plunged ahead and read his remarks (he was nervous, as nearly all of us are at the moment), his failure to alter his comments to adjust to the introduction told everyone present he was not going to be great at thinking on his feet. Even worse, his boss sensed the appointee thought his own introduction had been inadequate! Of such acorns ....

Their relationship was never quite comfortable after those swearing in remarks.

Personal Staff

But you won't make that mistake, so let us skip the ceremony and subsequent reception and turn immediately to organizing your staff and your routine. We start with your personal staff (the Secretary, Administrative Assistant, etc. in your immediate office, who are going to be particularly attentive to your every whim). Depending on the level of the job to which you have been appointed, you may have a secretary or two, and, in Defense, one or more military assistants or "aides."

I need to say something now which you probably don't cur-

rently believe, but hopefully, by the time you finish this book, will understand and accept. Nearly everyone in the Career Civil Service (and Military) strictly observes the rule, "The King is dead, long live the King."

Their loyalty is to America and the Department, not to your predecessor. They will love, respect and follow you unless you prove unworthy, and then they won't love and respect you anymore. As soon as the previous occupant resigned, or the election results were in, they started mentally adjusting to the new team. Operate as if you believe this and you will be off to a flying start. Alternatively, treat your inherited staff the same as you would political "enemies" and you are going to unnecessarily stumble, and maybe even fall. More than once.

First, let's worry about your administrative assistant or personal secretary. He or she is the individual who is going to keep your schedule, (inevitably) act as your gatekeeper and be the first person many of your guests meet. (Mine was a woman, so I am going to use female pronouns.) If she is pleasant and helpful, she will be the welcoming presence or telephone voice many people in the Department, Washington and elsewhere, will grow to think they know better than they know you. Her professionalism will become part of your own reputation.

Obviously, you need someone who knows the new (to you) territory or can learn it quickly. Personally, I hope you didn't decide to bring someone with you for this job. It certainly is permitted if you are a sufficiently senior appointee. But is it wise?

You will have all the latitude in the world in this selection, but in most cases I recommend you interview some of the professional administrative assistants already employed by the Department and endeavor to find one you like.

Why? There are two big reasons. To begin with, your main disadvantage at the beginning of your tenure is that you do not know your staff, the staffs of your new associates, or the idiosyncrasies of the processes (routine things such as how the mail is handled, letter and memo formats, how you get someone into the building, arrange parking, etc,). Your personal staff is going to be invaluable in advising you on what has been the normal process, who has special knowledge on a particular subject, and to whom you should be talking in the other parts of the Administration, in Congress, in the industry, and in the special interest organizations whose attention is focused on your Department. Why handicap yourself by bringing in someone who starts out as clueless as you are?

Secondly, you are in a new job, probably unlike any you have previously held. You are going to need to grow to fulfill the promise the President saw. At the beginning (at least), you need to be a sponge for new knowledge and perspectives. You are bright; you do not need the crutch of someone who is familiar with your old habits and limitations (and may therefore inadvertently hinder your growth). In addition, you don't know if he or she can adapt to the new environment. If you bring someone from the "outside," it is the rare associate who is ever going to come in and tell you if your trusted assistant is hurting your performance or reputation.

I have seen "an old friend" of a new boss come in to be his Administrative Assistant and promptly display their own nervousness by being discourteous to key congressional staffers they didn't happen to recognize, or unnecessarily abrupt to important members in the Bureau. I even watched one take the telephones out of the outer office, so she wouldn't be disturbed by guests making or taking calls while waiting to see her boss! If your personal secretary is a regular civil servant, someone is going to quickly tell you if she is not performing, and you can quickly get a replacement. If you brought an "old friend" with you, you are going to hear nary a word.

The job is hard enough.

The next key individual on your personal staff is your Executive Assistant and/or your Senior Aide. This is probably your most important selection (if it is a military billet, Defense or the Service(s) will nominate several candidates). While making the decision, recognize that this person is going to be a key access avenue into many facets of the organization. In many circles (not political ones) in your Department or Agency, he or she is going to be indistinguishably identified with you. He or she is also going to represent you in some meetings you cannot attend, be the oracle on what you "really think," and spend more time with you than anyone, including your significant other, over the next few years.

This brings up another important point. If anyone on your personal staff does not meet your expectations, replace them. Firing anyone is difficult, but your personal reputation and performance are at stake. You have a limited amount of time in the position and you serve "at the pleasure of the President." You can be replaced in a heartbeat. Thus it is important that you have a team which can support you in effectively carrying out your agenda.

You need to value and trust your personal staff, and if you don't, there are tons of less sensitive or different skill set jobs waiting for them elsewhere in the Department. Don't rob yourself of an asset you need by continuing to work with someone in whom you no longer have confidence.

All the aides are volunteers for the assignment, so being fired is one of the risks of their job, just as it is yours. You can't worry about the impact which dislocating them will have on their careers. Being replaced as your aide will not destroy an individual, because everyone recognizes aide jobs to political appointees present the opportunity for friction that may well not be the fault of the aide. Getting fired doesn't help him or her professionally, but it is not the kiss of death. After all, you are a political.

If you are appointed after the Administration is underway, as so many of you will be, you will probably be met by the political and career (and military, if in Defense) staff left behind when your predecessor packed out his office. They may well be the exact people you want, and they certainly should know how to get routine things done routinely. But if you are uncomfortable with any of them, work with the personnel shops to assemble a new team (they will prepare a package of reliefs for you to pick from). The political, career and military organizations do not want you to be unhappy and they also do not want to leave one of their people in a no win situation.

If you have a military assistant, do not obsess over the "efficiency" or "fitness" reports you will be required to write on the military officers serving you. You should do your best to make sure the report rewards a job well done, but there are subtleties in each Service's report and culture you can never hope to grasp, and the skill sets for Washington duty may be different from those valued in the field. If you have a truly exceptional officer that you want to see rewarded, seek the advice of a senior flag or general officer from his or her Service. With his or her aid, you can have an impact.

Without this senior officer assistance, it won't make a great deal of difference what you write. Flag officers working for you are going to go elsewhere based on their past service reputation, and junior officers are normally reassigned where their previous performance indicates is appropriate. The Service promotion and selection boards recognize you only see a very limited number of officers and find it difficult to compare them accurately to the large number of their peers elsewhere in the military.

In the case of the civil servants working for you, the situation is different. These are not uniformed warriors, and the skill sets they apply in your behalf are representative of their full value to the Country. At the same time, there are nuances in all reporting systems and this one is no exception, so I recommend seeking the advice of the senior career civil servants. For example, when I annually ranked the ninety Senior Executive Service (the top six grades of the civil service system) individuals reporting to me, I convened two panels consisting of the political appointee supervisors and the career civil servants in the top two Senior Executive grades. (I did two panels so that no career civil servant had to comment on his own ranking.)

In each panel, we spent several hours candidly discussing the performance and relative ranking of each of the individuals, with me acting as the activist to encourage others to talk about teamwork (strengths or problems), initiative (presence or lack thereof), etc., and each supervisor defending his or her proposed rankings. This process served to acquaint supervisors with perceived problems others observed in their people. The information from the panel deliberations was inevitably eye opening for one or more supervisors and assisted/grew their own personnel management skills, as well as giving them a list of items they should either simply note, or actively help their subordinates improve.

The process also produced a ranking which the whole group believed imminently fair. This is organizationally important since sizeable cash bonuses and prestigious awards follow for those ranked at the top, and you may not want to award someone who, while he may be fooling you, everyone else considers simply a fool. Even more significantly, the fact that we held the panels, and devoted hours to discussing the Senior Executive Service members, sent messages to the entire career civil servant corps that each was valued and their performance was important to both the Administration and the Department.

Let's turn now to the selection and training of your Executive Assistant and/or Senior Military Aide. This is the most important person you will train. You will not have the time to take every call or talk to everyone who thinks they have information you need. Your Senior Aide must act as your right arm and "attention director." This person must know what you think, what you are trying to accomplish and how you plan to do so, in order for her/him to do their job effectively. (My last Executive Assistant was a woman, so I will consistently use feminine pronouns for reading ease).

She needs a context in which to listen to people, read messages, attend meetings, walk the halls, talk to her peers, and know which things to bring to your attention. She also needs to feel confident that she can be completely frank with you. It is critical that you know what she or others think isn't working. There will be no shortage of people who will be dedicated to kissing your gorgeous cheeks (as improbable as it seems, after confirmation there will be a queue). Your Executive Assistant should not be in that line.

I also used her (as well as my Administrative Assistant, as one was usually present in the office) to review my emails. In many jobs, the computer volume will be great and include messages that are important because of the originator, or their context, or both. Some need to be brought immediately to your attention, no matter what you are doing, and you (hopefully) will frequently not be at your monitor! You need someone you trust, who is current on the issues and your activities, to carefully monitor this information source. More on emails in the next chapter.

The final key person on your immediate staff is the person who handles the paperwork. A tremendous amount of paper and information will cross your desk/computer screen. All of the decisions and coordinations which come to your desk are difficult. Simple problems are handled by someone else at a lower level. At the same time, the world and events move at a fast pace in Washington, and a decision delayed is a decision made. If you don't want the particular result that comes from a decision delayed, then you must act. If you don't want the rest of the Department team to actively look for ways to avoid involving your office, you and your staff must make timely decisions. Don't get the reputation as a bottleneck. The person controlling your paperwork is the only one who knows whether or not you and your staff are being timely. That individual(s) must know you care.

I once had a Congressman call to complain of an unanswered letter he had written me two months earlier. The answer to the Congressman was easy – someone had made an administrative error which affected one of his constituents, and we were going to make the constituent whole. Or at least the answer would have been easy if we had answered it two months ago! Sixty days is a long time for resentment to fester. Now I had to waste a lot of my time on personal apologies and the Congressman would still suspect I was incompetent.

When I investigated, I had a whole pot full of internal problems. Had I seen the original letter? No. My staff had shunted it off to be answered (and the bureaucracy had difficulty finding the precise words to describe why someone had made an error but that no one should be admonished). Whose fault? Mine. A political appointee should see every letter a Member of Congress or Senior Government Official writes. They are not writing to a staff person. The writer knows your office. He also knows the President's name.

When a letter from a Member is received, either you call him/her to say you received the letter and what you are doing to answer it, or you send a note back that day giving the same information. Then you track the progress of the response. I recommend you see a printout or computer screen each day which has this data so you can refresh yourself. There is nothing less fun that meeting a Member on the street or in a hearing, and having him mention, or wave in your face, a piece of paper which has not been answered, while you futilely search your blank memory bank.

By the way, my office was so screwed up we did not even have a system to track Congressional correspondence. I was humiliated, but I didn't fire anyone. This was my fault. Probably they had a system at some time in the past, but obviously I had failed to sufficiently sensitize them as to the critical importance of this routine task. Take heed. Unless you pay attention to correspondence at the beginning, and then routinely follow up, you also will be professionally embarrassed.

Office Management

Before we leave the subject of aides, how much can you trust them? It would be foolish to believe they are immediately completely loyal to you. While you can have an input, when push comes to shove, you do not have absolute control of their promotions or their next assignment. (As we are going to discuss, you will probably only be a memory in the next Administration.) In addition, especially early on, you do not understand the culture and values which have been inculcated in your aides.

There are two ways to approach this. One is to deliberately exclude your aides from issues in which you suspect his/her bureau or military service has a significant interest. I have seen (too) many offices run in this manner. The obvious problem with this approach is that you are not getting the value of their personal backgrounds and intellectual capabilities. You also are not training them to see the issue from your perspective and thought process. Conseuently, they will never be full members of your team, and you will have misused a valuable resource.

The second method, which I strongly favor, and have used several times, is to run a relatively "open" office. In an open office, you are as free with information as your boss permits and you encourage your staff to help you as a true team. If you run an open office, you will help the career organizations quickly learn who you are and what you are about. The downside of this approach is that your expressed views may find their way back to the aides' career organization more quickly that you might like. A little self-discipline can help here. On the other hand, the quick flow of information has its advantages.

Let's take a specific example, taken from Defense, but applicable to relations with all career staffs. I have gotten excellent results by *encouraging* my military aides to discuss what I was doing on issues involving their parent Service, thus building the aides' standing and value within that Service. After awhile I found the information flow became a two-way street and I received at least as much information as I was transmitting. Which is good! More information facilitates better decisions.

If you disagree with the military on an important issue, you should want the military to have time to convince you of your error. They are professionals. They have spent as many as thirty years in their profession. You may have the authority to make a decision, but you should be very interested in giving those military professionals (or career servants) every opportunity to make their case. In those situations where the military's position doesn't make sense, when you push back, you will eventually get to someone more senior who can better explain the true rationale for a position. Then you can make your judgment.

If you don't provide the opportunity for the military and career staffs to educate you about their position, you are going to find them progressively less cooperative when you need their support. If the issue is important to them, and you decide against their advice, you are going to hear about it from the Service's friends in Congress. So you might as well take the time to hear all the arguments before your decision, and refine your thoughts (and assemble your allies) now.

By the same token, you want the opportunity to communicate your thinking and positions on the issues. An open office can help. It gives you an informal exchange channel. Having your staff pass on your concerns is frequently more effective than personally calling up the Chief of Staff of the Service each time you sense your positions are not completely aligned. On the few occasions when I did not want something known right away, I ordered the aide not to repeat it. The military understands the chain of command and lawful orders. I was never disappointed.

Political Appointees

There will also be political appointees on your staff. When the White House and the senior leadership ask you to interview these people, do so seriously. These are usually very capable people who are the next generation of Senate-confirmed appointees. So pick them and train them well. If there is a major personality conflict, perhaps another place would be better for them. On the other hand, each one offers the opportunity to bring you his or her own unique experiences. Once they become part of your team, they will need more routine "face time" than a career civil servant, for they frequently know the Department and the players even less well than you do, and without your help they may feel lost or misfiled by the "system."

Just as each of your aides starts out with some divided loyalties (between you and their Bureau or Service), each member of your political team has his or her own political mentor – in the White House, on the Hill, or back in a State. They may start out thinking they are their own independent barony. To be entirely honest, each can be a challenge. Even more than with the career civil service staff, you have to convince them you are worth working with and deserve their loyalty. This is called leadership. They, on the other hand, need to learn to work with the rest of the political, career civil servant (and sometimes military) team. In many cases, they may have never been part of a team, and this is another reason they will require special attention from you. However, recognize that each political appointee is an opportunity, because he or she provides you an informal path back to their mentor.

I once interviewed a person looking for a civil servant political appointment, who had not "been right" for several other jobs. I took him, recognizing he would need special attention (one of the burdens of leadership) if he were to succeed. With some limited coaching, he became as good as or better than any of my career civil servants.

Did I mention he frequently played golf with the President, and had been the best man at the wedding of one of the Cabinet members? A lesser man than I would have been unable to ignore the opportunities those relationships might offer in accomplishing my Department's agenda. I am a lesser man.

Leadership Rules

1. The king is dead. Trust the career civil servants (and military) to be loyal to you and the new Administration. They are very talented and knowledgeable. If included, and properly managed, they will be of invaluable assistance.
2. Carefully select or accept your personal staff. Tell them clearly what you want. Ask them for help. If one does not perform, find another.
3. Devote special attention to Congressional letters. Pay attention to the person who is responsible for processing paperwork. His/her performance sends clear signals about you.
4. Recognize and use the communication avenues your aides offer for informal coordination with the career cultures in the Bureaus and Military Services.
5. Spend the extra attention that is needed on the more junior politicals assigned to your staff. Teach them and make them part of the team. Each brings his or her own unique capabilities. It is your responsibility to focus them on your agenda.

Chapter Three

ORGANIZING YOUR DAY

Once you have organized your office, you need to attend to getting your personal routine off to the right start. You are going to be busier than you ever thought possible. You will not have sufficient time for everything in your portfolio. You must husband time. Identifying those issues on which you will spend this precious resource will be critical to your success.

Meetings

With whom, how often and for how long?

Before considering your own meeting needs, you need to determine how to communicate effectively with your boss (last gender pronoun alert – I have worked for both male and female bosses, so the pronouns are going to vary hereafter). You will need to see your boss, talk to her, email her, or somehow communicate daily or more often so you keep in tandem, while concurrently leaving time to deal with your own schedule demands.

How often and when is first driven by your boss's routine. Does she hold meetings daily? At what time? What does she expect? Does she want the background of anything in that day's newspapers, if you haven't (hopefully you have) already given her a head's up? (Each Department will have a daily compilation, drawn from all the periodic publications, at home and abroad, of articles about Departmental-related matters. It is published early each morning. It's most avid reader is usually your boss.)

If the boss expects a meaningful discourse, then you need some method to ensure you are prepared before the meeting. A common method is to meet earlier with your own staff. Whenever the time of your meeting, remember that, in order to be prepared, whoever briefs you has to have begun work a couple of hours earlier.

Most people do their own daily meetings to prepare to meet the boss. It is probably the best, particularly if you are not exceptionally well grounded in your area of responsibility. On the other hand, there is always room for personal preferences. I asked my people to send me early emails or call or drop by before the time of my boss's meeting if there was something they thought the boss might be interested in that day. I also normally got in to the office in time to prepare my own thoughts and make the necessary telephone calls for added information. Then, I held my own routine staff meetings immediately after the boss's meetings, so I could pass on her insights and the consequential taskings.

I didn't want to hold multiple meetings with the same people (and waste their time), and I found my particular routine produced results more quickly and kept my staff more current as to the boss's desires that day. I did not want to be 24 hours behind. To each his own, but whatever routine you follow, take care to be sufficiently prepared so as to earn and keep the boss's confidence.

You have all been in lots of meetings before your first one in political office, but let me offer a thought. No matter how small the gathering, there is an audience watching your boss's interaction with you. You will acquire or lose authority based on how close and effective "they" evaluate the relationship. I believe the key to all workplace interpersonal relationships is focusing on the team output – for example, during a meeting with my boss, I would normally kickoff the issue (while the boss put aside what the President had just said to her on the telephone, gathered her thoughts and observed the audience), and then I became quiet while the discussion progressed and played to her strengths. Quiet doesn't mean asleep, for you are always mentally checking to determine if the evolving answer is consistent with the larger picture. When the meeting lags or closes, it is time to take care of the administrative details, such as dividing up the tasks, and assigning specific actions, responsibilities and due dates.

Edification

However you solve your boss's daily information demands, how are you going to run your own information meetings? There is a saying in the Navy that the difference between the Wardroom (the officers assigned) and the Chief's Quarters (the senior enlisted in the command) is noon meal. On a ship, all officers eat noon meal with the Commander. From his casual conversation, along with their food, they absorb a great deal of insight in how the boss thinks and reacts.

Your staff will benefit from the equivalent of the Navy's noon meal. They need to see what you think is important. They need to hear from you what your Department, Agency, Bureau or Service believes are the key issues for the near future and beyond. They need to observe how you react to tribulations, so they will not be fearful of reporting bad news, and be better able to identify what are real problems and what are not. They need to hear your corrections of others so they can alter their own course earlier next time. They need interaction with you to learn not only what you think, but how you think. They need to become comfortable with you as a leader.

The best leaders I have seen did a great deal of subtle teaching by thinking through problems out loud. By being confident enough to verbalize their own process, they allowed us to see the particular logic trail they first walked, as well as the critical assumptions. This process also exposed us to the ideas they discarded (and why), as well as to the aspects put aside for later consideration. It was great training! It was also an effective way in which to sponsor good teamwork. Not only did this allow those present to see the considerations which a more experienced mind evaluated, it also made our contributions more pertinent. We knew which assumptions were critical to his conclusions, and thus knew where to focus our own experience and thinking. This is another reason I am so wedded to the "open" office environment discussed in the preceding chapter.

The occasion of a staff meeting also generates a great deal of informal business before and after the meeting. Your staff is scattered. Some of them are not even physically located at the Headquarters. When they come together, they are naturally reminded of issues they should have discussed with one another, and advice they should have sought. Frequent staff (or sub-staff) meetings facilitate this informal exchange. But don't think you have to be deliberately tardy to these meetings in order to facilitate this exchange. Individuals who have something to coordinate will arrive early or stay late to talk. As I will repeat later – timeliness may not beat out cleanliness, but it is in the top four!

Attendance

At the same time, your staff is busy. Your will find your Department or Agency is chronically undermanned, and your staff will have more responsibilities than time or bodies. Long meetings in which various staff members are trying to impress you with their knowledge are morale killers for everyone. Inevitably, some of these windbags may be other political appointees whom you cannot change or correct. I never scheduled a staff meeting for longer than half an hour, to hold the show-offs in check, and I always ended the meeting on time. At the same time, I left 15 minutes after the meeting (hidden) in my schedule to follow up on individual conversations that needed to be completed (without holding the whole staff hostage). Personally, I tried to hold at least three full staff meetings (e.g. one representative from each key component) a week, and insisted on two. In many jobs, daily meetings are a must.

Try as you may to think of your whole staff as a team, the truth is that some staff members are more equal than others. When you decide who these individuals are, it frequently is a good idea to schedule weekly one-on-one, or one-on-few (if you are interested in ensuring interaction between their offices) meetings with those more-equal folks. Weekly meetings give these key people both the psychic recognition they deserve and also ensure they will take extra care in keeping you up to speed on their key concerns, plans and progress.

How many people should attend your meetings? Many political appointees seem consumed with the desire to limit information, and accordingly strictly — and excessively — minimize attendance (often to only those who don't know anything about the subject). I recommend you attempt to be as liberal as the size of the room can accommodate. This serves several purposes.

One is that people want to meet you and see you think. Without personal contact, you are only a picture on the wall by the building entrance. In addition, you are often being briefed on subjects of which you may have very little personal knowledge. Not only do larger groups help you in gathering information, facts and cultural inhibitions, they are also an opportunity for you to introduce new information to ears that may hear, and to "teach" a larger group how this Administration wishes to operate.

Secondly, you want as much information as possible on a subject, and frequently you can learn a great deal by observing body language around the room during the discussion. Personal interaction and observation is so key to my own management beliefs that I instinctively dislike video conferences simply because of the number of times in conventional meetings I have been alerted to a possible discrepancy when I saw a junior staffer's brow furrow while his boss was giving me a "fact." You can't receive body language signals through video links.

In general I believe not limiting the size of groups helps you maximize your professional impact. However, there are several exceptions. You should not have larger groups simply as a mirror for your own personal importance. Don't waste people's time just because you are a senior official.

Another exception is that there are people who are going to want to see you who themselves will be put off by larger groups, and your guests will not say precisely what they came to say with strangers present, even if it is only your Executive Assistant in the room with you. A good thumb rule with visitors from outside the Department/Agency is to limit the number of people you invite to the same number the visitor brings with him or her. In most cases you should certainly include your expert on the subject they wish to discuss.

The reason for the latter will become painfully apparent as soon as you have failed to do so once or twice. If your visitor is going to ask you to do something, and you agree, and you haven't included in the meeting the person who supervises that area for you, then when you turn to that worker bee to tell him what to do, you are going to have to waste your time repeating the conversation nearly word for word if you hope for him to have context. The complete success of recall is always iffy, even if your Executive Assistant also heard every word. It is also embarrassing to discover, after the meeting, that you have just agreed to something clearly undoable! I have done this. Include the expert!

There are also occasions when you are going to discuss things which you do not yet wish to share with anyone but your most trusted aides. Those meetings are fewer than you might think, as long as you can keep your mouth shut at the appropriate times in larger meetings. Remember that no one is ever putting thumbscrews on you to force you to be politically stupid in front of someone who might report your miscue. A little self-discipline can be a useful trait.

Going down the Hall

Now, when your boss calls, who do you take with you? Normally, no one. On the other hand, for planned meetings, when a particular subject is going to be briefed or discussed, it is often useful if you take the subject matter expert along. He or she will be pleased by the recognition, and will feel honored. In addition, it is always nice to have some facts at the table. Of course, if the subject is one on which your boss expects <u>you</u> to have become an expert, it might be best to think a minute about whether you actually need someone physically present. You might just need to make sure the right person(s) can be reached by telephone.

Actually, as a good leader, you want as many of your people as possible to be present in any meeting discussing their subject, and you want all of them to feel positive about the organization and your boss, whom you know to be great. But take care — nearly every boss is going to feel overwhelmed if you traipse in, unexpectedly accompanied by a half a baker's dozen staffers, and one of your people may subsequently be embarrassed when the boss's assistant invites them to do a Cinderella and sit outside. It is better to take one or a maximum of two people and rotate your attendance selection over time, as necessary to accomplish your "stroking" goals.

One special note: many organizations have someone who just cannot resist keeping his or her mouth shut, not just when he has an "Eureka" idea, but every single day. If you have one of these special individuals, then think several times, and then reconsider, before you ever expose them to your boss. It is in no one's interest for the boss to believe one of your people is a fool. He may ascribe that problem to your leadership.

What happens when you can't attend the boss's meeting yourself? You are going to find you cannot attend every meeting you would like to, nor every meeting you probably should. Which ones do you go to, and whom do you send as your representative if you can't attend? The temptation is to be present at as many of your boss's meetings as you possibly can. This will not work. There is too much to do, and too many problems to be addressed, for political appointees to spend the day sitting unneeded at the right hand of their boss. There are no extra appointees in any Department. Unlike the Yankees, you do not have a deep bench.

At the same time, your presence or absence at a meeting sends a clear message about your priorities. I have seen very senior officials fail miserably simply because they tried too hard to meet the roll call at each of the boss's meetings. At the same time (which is why this is such a difficult and judgmental issue), I have seen others fail to become trusted team members because their absence sent the message that they didn't care about their boss's priorities. Choosing the correct fine line to walk is frequently your very first tough decision and no alternative is ever right for all times. Sometimes your boss is going to need or want you to essentially act as a staffer for her and you are going to do so in order to enhance your future access to her as well as your stature in the Department/ Agency. Other times, you need to gently disengage and proceed about your previously assigned duties. No crisis lasts forever.

When you choose not to be there, I have no special advice as to whom you send in your place. I always sent the appropriate subject matter expert, and expected him or her to fill me in on what occurred when appropriate.

Conflicts and Goals

Now that you have gone through all of this planning, I have some bad news. Your schedule is going to get all bollixed up.

Think about the breaking news in a week's worth of the *New York Times*. Many of these National and World events are going to directly impact one or more of the officials in your Department and, as a result, have an unforeseen and yet predictable impact on your meticulously planned schedule. If the event doesn't directly affect you, then possibly you may need to pick up some of the workload for the official it does affect. Alternatively, one of the CNN news flashes may have also caused a blip on the radar screen of someone in the White House, resulting in a quickly called Eisenhower (Old) Executive Office Building meeting, and you are the designated Department representative. Unfortunately, not being prescient, breaking news wasn't on your schedule.

Face the facts. Your schedule is going to change. But since you have been forewarned, you are going to leave some flexible time in every day's schedule in order for your secretary to move meetings around as your schedule adjusts to accommodate world events. Leave more time when Congress is in town; Congress can be as demanding as several mischievous countries.

Also make time on your schedule for your personal agenda. Having talked with other politician appointees, you know that, in order to be effective, your personal agenda has to be no more than three or four items long, and even then you will be hard pressed to accomplish any of them before your tour is done. But making a list is the easiest step. The tougher part of success is laying a proper groundwork and staying focused. Nothing changes in Government without concerted effort over a long time. Your list will remain in a desk drawer, unchecked, unless you regularly devote schedule time to its accomplishment.

Telephone Calls

You also need schedule time to return emails and telephone calls. You are going to get a great number of telephone calls from people who expect their calls to be promptly returned. Many issues in Washington are very time sensitive. No matter what guidance you give your secretary, there is always some important person or issue he or she is not going to recognize. You cannot have meetings scheduled back-to-back-to-back all day and expect to have the time to think, much less check your telephone log, recognize the timely importance of the caller, and return those particular calls. On the other hand, if you don't return the right calls promptly, you are going to unnecessarily irritate someone you need in order to get your job done.

My rule was that I was only to be interrupted for calls from my immediate family, The Secretary, Members of Congress and a list consisting of four names in the Administration. That left a great number of important people who expected a call back quickly.

One way to do this is to insist that the "call list" of phone calls you need to return is kept in the middle of your desk, so that you can check it between meetings, and either return the call, direct someone else to call back (getting information or telling the party when you will personally return the call), or make a conscious decision to return the call later. When you are on travel, your assistant should get this information to you as feasible during the day.

On Time

In addition to leaving yourself time to return calls, you need to ensure your schedule leaves you time to be **on time**. Each Administration routinely operates to the minute. Routine lateness is considered aberrant behavior.

If you are habitually late, in addition to sending a signal of how little you value everyone who meets with you, you are also screwing up all of their schedules, and the ripple effect is considerable. A senior official ten minutes late at the beginning of the day will, by the end of the workday, have adversely affected the schedule of everyone who works for him. Those affected will all know, and resent, the person who "dissed" them, even if it is the President, himself. I worked for one political appointee who was always late. Within a month, his reputation throughout the Department had been harmed. Over time, when, after many subtle hints, his behavior didn't change, he was actively disliked. He was smart, decisive and could get things done. It didn't matter. All anyone talked about was how he was always late. Be on time. Tardy behavior impacts your effectiveness.

There is also nothing more discourteous than leaving a group of people, or even one, hanging in your outer office while you finish up a meeting or make a telephone call. *(On the other hand, if you have to call someone immediately back, and you (or your assistant) so tells the group while (not after) they are waiting, and you keep the phone conversation short, the group will understand).* It is Washington.

All of the people who meet with you are important people in some sphere. They will resent being treated like serfs. Everyone in Washington values their time (this is true nearly everywhere, but it is almost a religion inside the Capitol beltway). Time is scheduled in quarter hour blocks and valued in minutes. I recently called on a senior official, told her what I had come to say and got her response and guidance in return. I immediately got up to leave. She looked with surprise at me, then at the clock on the wall, and said, with a smile starting to grow on her face, "Dave, you just gave me seven minutes back. You are the first person in a week who has given me time back for myself."

Too many people seem to want to bask in the "glow" of any senior official's office. Get in, state your business and get out. You will find you walk through the door more easily the next time.

Some (another official I asked to read this) would say this latter is too firm a rule. It's true that you need to gauge the tenor of the conversation and the atmosphere before getting up and walking out. Some senior officials may want you as a sounding board for another particular issue and would value some extended conversation. Or they may simply want some time for idle conversation with a fellow political appointee. This is a judgment call. On the other hand, it's just like a first date in high school – you want to be out the door long before she begins to want you gone. I recommend you bias your assessment with the knowledge that anyone senior is at least as busy as you.

Paperwork

You also are going to need some time to do the paperwork that requires your personal attention. How you handle this is dependent on your own personality and method of working. Some officials schedule regular time at the beginning and/or end of the day during which a staff member explains the background of the issue and answers necessary questions or takes notes of the additional information you need before making a decision. Many of these papers are routine, and just need someone of your seniority to sign or approve. On the other hand, you are frequently the first person to review a particular issue with the background and perspective to understand the political or larger national issues involved, and the other ephemeral issues which must be considered.

Also it is important to realize that once a day, or maybe twice a week, an issue paper will cross your desk that has been well-staffed by one or more of your most trusted individuals, and **the answer is completely wrong**! I do not know how the good managers seem to unerringly pull these particular packages out of the pile and lay them aside for further personal attention, but they do, *and you must*, if you are to be effective. No matter how good your staff, do not take paperwork for granted! You have value to add in this process.

While you are reviewing paperwork, and scribbling the occasional marginal note, never forget the Washington rule – never write anything you would not want to read in the Washington Post or Times. Unless it is deliberate, resist any impulse to write something which might be construed as critical of an Administration policy, another official, or anyone in Congress. No matter how true, funny or incisive, the words will read poorly with the President's or Secretary's breakfast eggs.

Of course, you trust everyone who works with you, but trusting them with your political effectiveness is going a bit too far. It is terribly hard to control fax machines, and if you never anger anyone on your staff, you are probably not showing up for work often enough.

I have a friend who thought he understood this potential problem, so he always wrote his candid and pithy comments on separate pieces of paper which he then clipped or (posted) to the document. His system was that his staff could read his true feelings, chuckle, remove them and throw them away before mailing the document on.

A perfect system, with no record to be "discovered" under the Freedom of Information Act, and my friend could freely vent his true feelings on all issues, from people to policy. You would be surprised how many managers cleverly invent a similar system.

Of course, there was a day that the Secretary called and asked for a document concerning a buddy he was hiring, and a secretary from another office, who was sitting in for my friend's secretary's lunch break, faxed the Secretary's office the document just as it had come out of my friend's office, complete with the "posted" note describing what my friend _truly_ thought of the Secretary's worthless buddy.

There are dangerous holes in any system which seeks to "erase" written comments.

Emails

You are going to get a great number — which is good. Short emails are frequently all that is needed and are infinitely better than playing telephone tag. But, I also never buried myself in front of a computer screen. You need to get prompt information, but you are a "Political," and you are the one who should be capable and skilled at working human/personal interactions to develop solutions. This is not English class. Brilliant compositions do not carry the day against the enemies of light. You need to talk to other decision-makers, discover their core expectations, and shape broad or specific solutions which can work. In Washington, this isn't done at a keyboard. Your Administrative Assistant should be the one getting eye strain.

If you establish rules, read fast, and are brutally efficient with your time and your responses, you may be able to read all your emails yourself, although this work will often get completed outside "normal" working hours unless you are superhuman. Here, you need to adjust your routine to the volume in your particular Department/Agency and job. In some very heavy jobs, if you are a mere mortal, you will want someone, very bright and trusted (probably your senior assistant) on your staff to screen the emails and answer those he or she can appropriately do. I had my Administrative Assistant and Executive Assistant set up to read my email. The former in order to alert me to those requiring immediate action because of their content or originator, and the latter so that she was keeping abreast of the issues. Keeping up with correspondence is truly a team effort.

On another aspect of personal time management, some of your people are going to want to send emails with attachments. I made the rule to my staff that I would not read attachments. There are exceptions, but normally, <u>any communication that needs attachments should be sent by paper</u>. If you do not establish some rule, the inbox on your computer is going to become impossibly clogged, and important, time critical, notices are going to go unread.

I recognize this last "rule" is at least controversial, and other politicals may have handled this problem by either having their secretary print out all attachments, or by doing so themselves, and then reading the attachments during down times such as when riding in a car or sitting in your boss's outer office, waiting for a meeting. However, I disagree. I established the rule as stated above to also take care of the staffer who can't tell what is important, and thus hits the "insert" function key on a whole article, when only a paragraph or phrase would do – that person needs to learn to compose on paper.

I also have worked with many people, who, in order to cover their inability to discriminate between the wheat and the chaff, load a two page memo (hard copy or email) with reams of attachments. Later—when one of the myriad of issues in the tree of paper becomes important – this personality type inevitably washed their hands with the phrase, "I told you about that!"

My staff was instructed that I wasn't quick enough to pick up on innuendoes in papers and emails. Unless they had previously clearly explained the location, triggering mechanism and danger of a potential minefield, preferably in a short email, then I did not consider myself either warned or well-staffed.

I didn't read attachments.

One final note on emails. Whether or not there is a legal expectation of privacy, there is no such political expectation. Each year in Washington, there is a number, longer than the President's Christmas list, of people who regret, painfully so, something they put in an email. I once sent to one person a criticism of a policy, and received an information copy of the same comments, accompanied by comments about some of my close relatives, which had literally traveled around the world, with several intermediate stops, within 72 hours. (I survived only because the organization decided I was correct and the policy was subsequently changed – but I had inadvertently created an unnecessary situation for myself.)

Emails are essential means of communication, but, no matter what the confidentiality or classification of the net you think you are on, as the old ditty goes "Take care what you say of your seniors, be the words spoken softly or plain, lest a bird of the air tell the matter, and so shall you hear it again."

Classified Documents

Remember there are strict rules for taking classified materiel out of a designated area. No matter how far behind when I decided to quit for the day, I never took classified material home to work upon. The opportunity for disaster is just too great.

My most memorable example of this involved a friend who drove to New York to attend a Broadway play with his wife. As they got out of the car, he saw a classified sealed document (it was even numbered, so distribution could be both controlled and reconstructed) which had apparently slid out of his briefcase sometime before and wound up under the driver's seat. Thinking quickly, he had his wife remove her coat, wrapped the pamphlet in it, and left the coat on the floor of the car.

They were about a block away when they heard the window of the car break, and my friend turned to see a thief race off down the street with his wife's mink coat under his arm. Surprisingly, the thief was caught within a few hours by an officer of the law, who found the classified information untouched. Fortunately for national security, the officer immediately and personally took the unopened document to the New York Chief of Police. Unfortunately for my friend, the Chief of Police immediately called **his** close friend, the Secretary of the Department.

My friend decided to seek other employment.

Thinking Time

Thinking and reflection are always important. If you do not insist, your schedule will fill up faster than Miss America's dance card at a Shriners' convention. You are dealing with important, complicated issues; you need time to think of what you haven't done, who you haven't talked to, and possible options that haven't been explored. An overly full schedule is not a problem which can be dealt with once and remain solved.

Your Administrative Assistant will be under great pressure to add a "must have" meeting here and there. You have to balance that by exerting a little backpressure of your own. About every three months look at your schedule and see what sort of unnecessary meetings have become routine. Then, evaluate whether or not you are spending enough time thinking, walking the halls, talking to your people at *their* desks, and planning for the future. Do the necessary corrective schedule pruning and gardening.

Leadership Rules

1. Time is your most precious resource. Control it.
2. Problem solve aloud to train your people. It is an effective tool in making your team work better.
3. Answer telephone calls (and emails) promptly. The caller may have the answer you need, but set up a system so that neither communication takes over your life. The President hired you to be a political problem-solver, not an answering service or a computer geek.
4. Be on time. Others have the same Rule 1.
5. Save time to think, as well as to talk to your people about their lives.
6. Do paperwork promptly and thoughtfully.
7. The Washington Rule. (Don't say, do, or especially write, anything you would not be comfortable with your Mother, and the President, reading in tomorrow's newspapers).

Chapter Four

BUILDING THE TEAM

You have now organized your personal assistants, set out some parameters for day-to-day operation and begun to better know your staff. Before we discuss how to position yourself to be successful in the government-wide bureaucracy, let's finish up discussing your Department or Agency's Team. In addition to the principal organizations in your Department, don't forget the "staff" groups: the Congressional Relations people, those in Public Affairs and the attorneys.

Congressional Relations

You have already met the Congressional Relations people, and you need to continually build upon and reinforce those ties. These individuals will help you fulfill your role as a "point" person with Congress. Not only will they provide advice, but they can recommend whom to see and then advance, set up, and accompany you on trips to the Hill. You don't want to spend thirty minutes wandering around the Rayburn building only to find out no one in a Congressional office knows why you are there.

Public Affairs

You are going to learn to appreciate the Public Affairs personnel. If you work with them when you are directed, or decide, to give an interview, they are going to give you prior advice on both the interviewer as well as the sensitivity of the subject (Who else has lately said what about the same issues.) They also will sit in on and record your interviews. The good ones will assist you in staying on message and, very importantly, help avoid an inadvertent sound bite.

General Counsel

There are lawyers on, or assigned to, each staff. They get routine guidance and supervision from the Department/Agency/Service General Counsel (and sometimes Justice). Your attorney relationship is one that deserves special cultivation. Laws and precedence in Washington are the established boundaries for problem-solving. Since many of the issues which come across your desk require special knowledge, no matter what your background, legal assistance will be invaluable in quickly exploring the limits of these boundaries. To get this done, your attorney needs to be part of your problem-solving meetings. He, she or they, may well identify different aspects or facts of the issue at hand. This will, in turn, offer you different options.

Political appointees are frequently attorneys in real life, so you may personally know how lawyers are trained in evaluating problems. If you are not an attorney, make special efforts to ensure you are properly using this special resource. You are going to have lots of unique problems, and attorneys can be great sounding boards.

It is easy, particularly early in your tenure, to exclude your attorney, either by commission or omission, from meetings he/she should attend. Don't fall into this benign neglect trap!

In the end, attorneys are going to draft many of the papers upon which your decisions will be debated and judged. Capture them, and their assistance, up front. The good ones are going to come up with ways you CAN accomplish your goals at the least risk, rather than spending all their time telling you why you CAN'T do it. Unfortunately, apparently not all law schools get this precept clearly across to their graduates, so you may need to sensitize your own on what you expect. If you find you can't work well with your attorney, get another, just as you would replace your executive assistant.

Inter-Agency Stakeholders

The next step is to build relationships with the other political appointees. You will find that appointees come from all walks of life and political persuasions. It is a large country. Often you will have never previously met. Now you are all on the same Team. Just as it is in many other organizations, sometimes the most influential people do not have correspondingly splendiferous titles. Thus you need to pay attention to individuals' past personal relationships with other people in the Administration, as well as the organizational chart.

In addition, in each Department, Bureau and Service there were old reorganizations which never completely "took." You can rest assured that even in your Department there are somewhere still remnants of responsibilities that were never perfectly merged, and the seams of overlapping responsibility remain. Just as in baseball, those seams can produce friction and friction is the only component needed to generate a curve ball.

Overlaps, discontinuities and curve balls are resolved by consultation and coordination. Fixing this is going to be one of your jobs, so you need to start calling on your appointee counterparts in the White House, and other Departments/Agencies, as well as those within your own area of responsibility in the rest of your Department. Sometime in the future you will need each of these individuals to be, if not personal friends, at least willing to take your calls. In addition, you want to know, as early as possible, where they have different views so you can plan to accommodate or work around "Team Issues." The inevitable friction between and among organizations with overlapping responsibilities is only resolved at your level. It is easier if there is a relationship between the princi-pals before the bell rings to announce the fight.

Why is this important? The two keys to getting things done in Washington, as you will glean from the following case studies, are identifying a capable individual to provide the leadership to drive a problem to a solution, and then investing time in prior consulta-tion before taking action. Someone has to lead, and you, as the political appointee, are going to get the bulk of these assignments for your area, but you must coordinate with others. Problems are not only complex, tough tribulations, but they frequently involve someone who is outside your own immediate Team. So, your civil servants are going to help you identify the different teams, and you are going to get to personally know the players.

Accessing Palace Guards

This is as good a time as any to talk about the nuts and bolts of establishing a relationship. The first step is to get on his or her calendar. This process starts with the person the other official has entrusted with his schedule. The schedule-keeper is colloquially known as the palace guard, or gatekeeper.

The key to dealing with palace guards is to recognize they are as easily influenced as the rest of us by the milk of human kind-ness. Too often their working hours may seem to them to revolve around fielding snide or nasty remarks from individuals who do not understand the time demands which the Department, and his/her responsibilities, put on the boss's schedule. You can get more access than you deserve by following three simple rules:

Learn the "Guard's" name, use it, and pay him/her the courtesy any person deserves;

Be credible about how important your issue is to the boss. (Is the issue truly important to him/her? Could it be done by an email or a note, or do you just feel the need for some face time?); and accurately access the time sensitivity issue. How soon do events demand that you see her boss? Don't imply an issue is urgent when it is not.

By strictly observing these rules, within a few weeks after I had decided that I needed frequent contact with another senior official, I could get that contact whenever I needed it nearly anywhere in Government. Many never learn the code, and they will remain standing frustrated, looking in, on the outside of both individual issues and the overall action. You can't be effective in Washington without access. Work to establish it.

Problem Solving In An Intergovernmental Environment

The public policy problems it will be your responsibility to solve are not only complex, tough issues, but frequently do not respect Department or Agency boundaries.

For example, in the area of export control, the Congress has given regulation authority to the President, who has passed this on by Executive Order to State, with Commerce and Defense having specific subordinate roles. Let's assume the Secretary of Defense wants to sell an airplane to Country X, in exchange for base landing rights there, but the agreement stumbles over an export control tripwire. The Secretary tells you to fix it.

It is obvious that you have to get State, Commerce and Defense together. Defense includes not only the offices of Policy and Acquisition in the Secretary of Defense's realm, but also each of the three Services, who have technical roles. State includes not only the Arms Control Bureau, but also the Ambassadors (via the Regional Assistant Secretary) who have to explain and check compliance in their countries.

In addition, you also have to get the National Security Council in the White House on board, since their predecessors passed the authority to State. And, of course, the appropriate committees from Congress must be consulted, since the regulation authority is based in statute. If you are listening carefully to your career civil servants, you might also recognize the prosecutorial portion of Justice is involved, since they are the enforcement authority for the regulations, as well as the Customs Bureau, since they furnish the inspectors that police these laws.

No matter how much the Secretary of Defense may want a change, not consulting, in advance, with all of these organizations, will doom accomplishment of your task – or at the very least slow progress down to a crawl. Change may be difficult in Washington, but that is why we have such talented political appointees! When other people or organizations have an interest in an issue it is commonly called, "standing." And all progress on an issue will be stopped cold the first time someone with standing says, "This is the first time I/we have heard of this problem."

They may be reflecting the literal truth; then again they may be disingenuous; they may know all about the issue and have no interest in cooperation. They may intend to fight you tooth and nail, and this is simply the first barricade they have thrown up, but it is an impenetrable one if you truly have not done prior coordination. Regardless of the basis for their objection, like T-ball, the rules of this game require that everyone have a chance to play. I have lost weeks or months, several times, by failing to follow this simple rule. So, when you are tasked to get something done, you need to know not only who has expressed an interest, but also all those organizations who can wave a piece of paper, no matter how old and yellowed, which implies they have standing. Sometimes this is not easy.

Let's take an example that starts in Defense to illustrate the dynamics of "standing." Assume that military housing is in your portfolio. Each of the Services is a stakeholder, with not only political people holding their own portfolios in each service, as well as involved career civil servants, but also senior military people, who frequently act as "politicals" during the periods between appointments. The Joint Staff is also interested in housing, even if it is ostensibly a non-war-fighting issue, because they support the Unified and Specified Commands and housing is a significant morale issue overseas.

While the normal Defense contact in the White House would be the National Security Council, housing issues have many additional constituencies on the Presidential staff, including the Office of Federal Procurement Policy. Since military housing is a significant user of energy, it also affects any of the Administration's "Green" initiatives and thus is definitely of interest to whoever is holding the Energy and equivalent of the National Economic Council portfolios. Military Housing may well be important even to the Director of the Office of Management and Budget.

On Capitol Hill, there could be several layers of interest. First, there are sub-Committees in both the House and Senate dealing directly with housing, and, therefore, Members of Congress and staffers who have worked these and associated issues for years. In our example, you will need early and frequent interaction with each of them.

Depending on the nature of the housing issue and its geographic significance, you may trigger additional Congressional interest. If you want to do something new, such as building more houses (or fewer), or merely to put meters on the gas lines of existing houses, you are also going to find a raft of other Members instantly interested. This is because housing in a particular area not only directly impacts the welfare of their military constituents, but also pumps new money directly into a community, its building contractors, and its work force.

And if you were thinking about adding gas meters, you also will attract the attention of any Member with someone in his home district that makes, or thinks he might be able to make, gas meters. Or alternatively, you may draw the interest of the Member with a constituent who thinks gas meters are dangerous, or even the national organization that worries that individual gas meters are a step towards a hidden Service Member "tax," since the meters would make it possible, in the future, to hold the housing occupant responsible for how much energy he/she uses.

This is not a fanciful example. I have engaged in all of these discussions with each of the aforementioned players.

There is a lot of "standing" in Washington. There are a great number of stakeholders. If you intend to be effective, you need to start meeting them.

Leadership Rules

1. You can't be effective in Washington without knowing the people involved. Know and build support within your own team. Go out of your way to meet likely allies, as well as your bureaucratic "opponents." Do it early. You will need the time to develop personal and political solutions to the friction areas you uncover.
2. Your attorneys are important resources who require special attention if their skills are to be properly employed. Take the necessary time to make this relationship work.
3. Palace Guards, Congressional Relations and public affairs are three "must know" groups.
4. Intergovernmental and departmental problems can not be solved, and remain resolved, unless there is a great deal of prior consultation with those who have standing on an issue. Identification of all the stakeholders is a particularly valuable Washington skill. Some, like vampires, won't show up until the sun goes down, which may be too late – for you. Use all the assistance you can muster in identifying them early.

Chapter Five
_____

A CASE STUDY — CHIPS AND PROCESSORS

The hard work you are doing to learn the rest of the Administrative team has a purpose – to make you effective in Washington. The more effective you become the more you can contribute toward solving National problems. This case study is an example which showcases the following leadership and management precepts:

  • *The exceptional leader can develop an environment which encourages his or her people to think unfettered by previous assumptions. (Facts are facts, but often "facts" are truly only assumptions, and some assumptions are flat wrong.)*

  • *Times change. Circumstances change. A good manager should expect answers to alter accordingly.*

  • *Consensus building in Government is a necessary, but time-consuming, task. In any period of a year or two, you will only have time to construct a few consensus edifices around the Washington reflecting pool. Choose your targets well.*

The Situation

The computer chip and processor industry is important to the economic well-being of America. In the last decade, this industry has been responsible for more than three out of ten of the new jobs in America. It has significantly improved our standard of living, and been the source of a disproportionate percentage of our exports. Semi-conductor technology enabled smaller, smarter weapons and powerful, code-breaking, computers for the Cold War. These gave our forces unique military advantages. To try to maintain this advantage, Congress established restraints (export controls) on what could be shipped out of the United States, depending on the relative "friendliness" of the particular destination and our ability to check the uses to which the export was going to be devoted.

The Congressional limitation was established based on the operating speed of the processors (how many millions of theoretical operations a processor could conduct in one second or, in the shorthand of the industry, MTOPS). Technology is hard to legislate, but Congress received testimony that it took a very sophisticated technician to wire more than four processors to work together, and laws were subsequently written based on this key limitation.

In the industry's early years, three Departments (Defense, Energy and NASA) funded much of the research and development in chips, processors and computers. However, as the commercial computer industry took off, Government support became unimportant, and Defense, Energy and NASA each began adapting commercial processors for their own use, rather than developing unique software applications.

Since new applications are found for chips every day in the vibrant commercial industry, there was plenty of venture and investment cash available to fund the competition that drives innovation. As a result, the designers and manufacturers in the computer industry routinely doubled the capability of their product every eighteen months. Soon, the industry was bumping up against the Congressional limits. Concurrently, with the end of the Cold War, the fastest growing processor markets were in the Far East, particularly in China. The computer industry believed existing export control legislation, which severely limited any exports to China, would inevitably cripple America's Silicon Valley.

The Problem

Could the United States afford to ignore these particular market forces? If so, would not the innovation and leadership in this industry simply move to countries where they were not constrained by US export laws, taking with them not only the jobs but also the technological revolution that had fueled the American prosperity of the 1990's? On the other hand, if the US export laws were to be revoked or changed, could not any country, friendly or not, then be able to develop its own new stealth bomber?

If processing power were the key to America's advantage, we had better think fast. The Christmas toys coming off manufacturers' lines contained more processing power than did the computers used to design the F-117, the world's first stealth airplane.

With no change in the law, did we need to alert everyone Christmas shopping to carry their American birth certificate? Did the stores need customers to fill out a form saying they were only giving electronic gifts to Americans living in America this season? Did we need to alert Customs to inspect baggage and packages going overseas? Perhaps we should ask for legislation against types of toy manufacture? Something had to be done!

Considerations

The basic hypothesis inherent in the Congressional limitations was that increased processing power was equivalent to technological innovation. Was that assumption valid? Let's examine it. There are three basic steps which lead to improving technological capability – design and manufacturing of the chips, design and manufacturing of the processors, and design and manufacturing of the computers. So where are the risks to national security?

It wasn't in the stepper machines, which place the little lines on the chips that give the chip its speed and power, since most of the stepper machines used by American chip manufacturers are already made overseas.

And it couldn't be in the processor, because many of the chips and processors are also manufactured overseas.

So what was critical? Was it the design of the processor for specific applications? Was it in the software which operated on the machine? Was it the software which had been developed to do a specific function (e.g., design stealth airplanes, run air-to-air weapon simulations, etc.)?

If the key were the "function" software, then perhaps we should control that and free the American computer industry to try their best to remain as the world leader. If they did so, as a practical matter, Defense, Energy and NASA always got the new products first, frequently years ahead of any other consumer. If, on the other hand, American export controls essentially handed large markets away and made the development of foreign "silicon valleys" economical, then Defense, Energy and NASA would lose the competitive advantage of having the first crack at applying the fruits of the industry.

The industry brought their concerns to the White House, State, Defense and Congress. Were their concerns valid? Was there a national interest at stake? Who should take the lead, review the adequacy of the status quo, and balance competing considerations?

Taking Responsibility

The Deputy Secretary of Defense recognized this issue was of critical interest to national defense. He volunteered to take the lead for the Administration. His method of attack was a classic good management technique for dealing with an important problem. He started scheduling luncheons and dinners with all the people he could think of who had standing or interest in the issue, as well as those people who were his "problem solvers." At these functions, he began asking questions. He did not propose a solution at this point. He was both gathering information and, more importantly, sending a message –"This is an important issue. I am interested. It is worth my time (and thus is worth yours). You are important (or I would not be including you and buying you dinner). Think about the problem. Please help me solve it."

He invited Members of Congress, including members of the opposition, representatives of the chip industry, and representatives from the Administration (National Security Council, State, Commerce, Justice, NASA and the National Security Agency), military officers involved in high technology projects, as well as technical and idea people from his own staff. He did not talk to these people as separate groups, but mixed them into small groups, spending personal time with each group, looking for synergistic understanding and idea generation.

Throughout, he was also trolling for individuals to pick up the leadership of the process — to evaluate, gather data and feel personally responsible. A person as senior as the Deputy Secretary does not have time to solve problems himself. He is always being interrupted by wars and the other details of running Defense. However, if anything is to change, the leader must keep sending signals as to how important this is to him until those around him take up the torch and begin running. Then he has to provide follow-up.

The most important follow-up is to keep sending a clear, re-enforcing message of this problem's significance. If it is important to you, and your colleagues know it, they will accordingly adjust their priorities. On the other hand, some managers spew forth a fountain of new ideas each day, and the competent people around them, who already have full plates, as well as their own set of priorities, may not be able to intuit the hierarchy of ideas. Therefore, if you truly want something specific accomplished, you must consistently send an ungarbled signal of your primary concern(s).

Now, how do you recognize the best solution when it finally is unveiled?

Throughout the process, the Deputy Secretary examined the proposed theories, not only through the prism of his own experience, but through review with the people from his "challenge groups." By inviting them to review solution possibilities, **not after he had decided,** but rather along with him, he used their knowledge and bureaucratic skills to sharpen his assessment. When a solution was found using this approach, many key decision-makers had already been part of the process, so their personal buy-in was assured, that of their friends and colleagues much more likely. Consequently, the Deputy Secretary was accordingly a long, long way along the path to Washington consensus. The collegial solution path, which seems so long in getting organized, reaches the real finish line much more quickly in the Capitol marathon.

The Solution

After several months a new concept of chip/processor/computer/ software security emerged. It wasn't the chips that were important. It wasn't the processors. It wasn't the power of the computers that was decisive to Defense, Energy and NASA. Instead, it was the limited number of unique software programs written to solve special military, security and space problems! Many of these programs have taken ten or more years and hundreds of millions of dollars to write. This software reflects the distinctive capital and intellectual investment of the American industry and Defense establishment.

The good news was that these programs were already classified and protected, and did not have invaluable commercial value which demanded they be shared with industry. For example, modeling the operation of the different fighter airplanes in the world, and the air-to-air and surface-to-air weapons and countermeasures, is a necessary tool to examining air conflict scenarios and improvements. However, it isn't useful in helping civilian planners predict ground and air transportation flows in the city of Los Angeles.

While there are data handling processes and tools in the program that might have commercial applications (and Game Boy, for one, would love to have the whole set!), it became obvious that the affected Departments and Agencies could protect their unique software without irrevocably damaging the American computer industry.

A solution along these lines was proposed to the White House, approved by the President, and a compromise reached with Congress.

This was a very significant change. The power of a computer chip, its "MTOPs," could be measured and thus regulated by bureaucrats through the export control system. "Security" on the other hand, is difficult to legislate, and how many people on the Hill (or anywhere else) understand specific software programs?

However, once the proposed solution was adequately reviewed and socialized, it was obvious that the current legislation and the export control system were protecting nothing of value, and were, in fact, detrimental to the continued development of the American chip and processor industry. The law was changed.

While perhaps interesting in itself, the real value of this case is the manner in which a leader managed to create an environment which developed a completely new or "out of the box" answer to a time-critical problem. I was there. No one came up with "the answer" at the first meeting, the second, or the fifth. When the process began, no one person knew all the relevant factors, even the technical ones. Ideas and proposals were advanced, researched, and discarded. Eventually the participants got down to reviewing the bedrock assumptions behind the previous export policy. What is national security? Is it comprised of both economic and military factors? What are we actually protecting? What are the elements of military advantage, and how do we best safeguard them?

Most managers never get "out-of-the-box" solutions because they are not sufficiently skillful leaders. Solution innovation comes from a new perspective of the basic facts. It can be the product of one instigator who conceives by himself, as Einstein did his relativity theory. However, history tends to indicate that original genius is in somewhat limited supply. One shouldn't run an organization expecting brilliance to come to your day-to-day rescue. And you well may not recognize a genius when he knocks on your door – he or she may well have misplaced their mastermind nametag.

A preferable way is to manage your organization to facilitate mere mortals in developing "out-of-the-box" solutions. To do this requires the leader to clearly identify the one or few problems he believes important, and then to encourage interchange between his people and different/new ideas from other organizations, cultures and individuals. The leader's personal involvement in the process is essential. He needs to show it is acceptable to challenge the old assumptions. He has to demonstrate, by his personal interest, that this problem is, and remains, important to him.

A good leader is one hell of a fine manager.

Leadership Rules

1. A good leader can facilitate innovation. It requires personal involvement, a readiness to question previous assumptions, and the willingness to search for ideas and concepts new to the organization.
2. Times change. "Facts" change. People learn. Answers should also metamorphasize.
3. Attacking a problem collegially builds consensus as the work is done. It is a great technique for working in our Nation's Capitol.

Chapter Six

CAREER CIVIL SERVANTS

You are going to come to rely heavily on the judgment, advice and work of the Career Civil Servants. While the political appointees are being nominated and confirmed, and doing the work of promoting and defending the Administration's programs, the career civil servants are managing the routine of making the Department run.

Skills

All civil servants change jobs as they acquire skills, or are assigned new challenges, but they change desks much less frequently than, for example, the Diplomatic Corps in State or the military in Defense. The career civil servants tend to stay in one area of expertise. Each normally has years of experience in his/her discipline. As such, they know why things were done a particular way in the past, as well as the options and obstacles to doing it differently.

At this point, if you haven't been in government before, you are going to be thinking, "So, if they are so talented, why are they working for the Government? They don't make that much money."

You are correct. You probably made a great deal more money in private industry, and, at the same time didn't (you will find) have nearly the responsibility many career civil servants hold. I asked a career civil servant the same question once. I knew he had worked as an attorney in private industry for ten years before coming into government. He looked at me, smiled, and said, "I like the client better."

He then went on to discuss how interesting the work was, with new intellectual and practical challenges daily crossing his desk. He liked the challenge. He wasn't denigrating someone who spent nine months, day and night, on the intricacies of a lawsuit for some damaged child against a negligent doctor, obtaining a divorce against an abusive spouse, etc. Correcting injustice can certainly be admirable work and financially very rewarding. But, after the first few years in private practice, my friend had found it boring. He wasn't bored working for America.

However, I believe the real key to his continued personal decision lay in his comment about the "client." The United States is a client you always feel good about representing. My friend has now worked for the Government for fifteen years. He says he has never been tasked to legally pursue a course of action he felt was morally wrong.

In the main, career civil servants are those individuals who discovered the attraction of working for Government earlier than the rest of us and settled in for the long haul. Their psychic reward of interesting and morally rewarding work compensates for the limited monetary remuneration. They are very good people.

My bet is that you also will find Government work both interesting and morally satisfying. So much so, if you are like many of the men and women in previous administrations, you won't return home to your old job when your political service is over. Instead, the temptation will be to find some way to continue to work with, or against, the people who are now "The Government."

Loyalty

Initially, you are going to wonder about the career civil servants, "Are they loyal to me?" There is a short, and correct, answer. Yes. You are the only one with the power to make the process run and get things done. They need you to do their jobs. Also, to be crass, with civil servants you have all the tools of personnel management in your own grubby hands. For the career civil servants who are direct reports, you are the one who sets their goals, writes their evaluations, recommends special or annual bonuses for exceptional performance, and decides who will and who will not be promoted. You have both the bunches of carrots as well as the hammer.

Career civil servants do not have divided loyalties. They do not have somewhere else to go within government at the end of a short tour in your Department or Bureau. They do not wear uniforms. Only rarely do they even have any friends in Congress. Thus, their dedication is to doing their present job to the best of their abilities. For example, in the Office of the Secretary of Defense, most civil servants have been working in various capacities within that office for many years. Their loyalty is to Defense. Since all the key decision-making jobs in Defense are filled with political appointees, the Defense civil servant is loyal to the Administration. They consider it their job to make this complex and enormous government run efficiently. Essential to their success is providing you good advice and doing excellent work.

Tasking

Career civil servants can do whatever you give them to do, within some practical limits. They can't do your job. Sometimes, when there are questions on routine process or you are not ready to expose to the Congress where a decision is going, you may ask a particular senior civil servant to testify on the Hill, but only in carefully constrained situations. They are not going to make any news, accept any blame, take a position or announce any decisions. Normally, civil servants are seen and not heard by the Congress and the Public.

Within the bureaucracy that is Washington, the civil servants are going to follow specific issues and let you know when you need to take action. They are going to brief and prepare you for meetings as well as for hearings and testimony. They are going to coordinate among offices, departments and agencies, with other countries' corresponding bureaucracies, and anyone else you direct.

It is the civil servants who are going to draft the papers and speeches to express your thoughts. They are also going to feed you ideas, answer your questions and monitor the bureaucracy's performance in your area of responsibility. In short, career civil servants are the worker bees and the middle management of the Department.

This is probably a good place to put in a special note. While you are instructing them, the civil servants are also going to teach you a great deal. Learning is a two-way street. Please don't assume you know everything, or that some of the concepts you first held, on the day you were sworn, should not be discarded or modified as you become aware of new facts. The civil servants have been working their responsibilities a long time. You should expect them to know the history, the rationale, and the facts of all facets of your Department/Agency/Bureau. They are your institutional memory. Use and learn from their experience.

Risk aversion. At the same time as we are touting their capabilities, the career civil servant has, in general, a specific shortcoming it is important you recognize. The career civil service includes very few risk-takers who are going to assault the bulwarks of a particular "organizational" position.

There are several good reasons for this trait. It is, in part, the result of the organizational control over promotion and assignment of the great majority of the civil servants. It is also caused by the permanence of the career presence in the Department, which is only partially disturbed by the passage of particular political appointees. Even in the long periods of one party control of the Presidency and Senate, the constant rotation of political appointees produces gaps, sometimes lengthy, in all positions except the Secretary. (Remember the delay inherent in any appointee confirmation?) These factors produce real risks for civil servants who don't play by the institutional rules. A civil servant, who takes a stand in opposition to a particular military service's position in the Pentagon, or to a Bureau position elsewhere, is in grave danger of not being promoted again. If he or she is in a position of significant responsibility and the organization considers the issue important, the career civil servant is headed to Siberia, if not when you turn your head, then certainly soon after you are gone. You, as a political appointee, must recognize this unstated essence of career civil service life. Don't ask an apolitical career civil servant to be the point for you. A career civil servant can help you make change happen, but should not be the advocate. That is your job. Ask for help, but when arguing for change, stand on your own feet.

I personally ruined several career civil servants' careers by capturing them up completely in a change I believed was important. They were very effective in moving the issue forward through the swamps and fires that are Washington. But I failed to shield them sufficiently, and when I left, and some in the next Administration disagreed with my goals or methods, the only people left to take the brunt of that displeasure were the career civil servants. They did.

Do seek the career civil servants' advice and counsel. Recognize that they can move mountains as representatives of your decision. But you need to always provide covering fire.

Let me make up an example. Assume you are in Office of the Secretary of Defense and have an office that monitors the Army's programs that develop, buy and maintain wheeled vehicles. Imagine the Army is developing a new big truck for hauling ammunition, supplies and people around the battlefield. You expect your civil servant responsible for this area to know nearly everything about the program: to know trucks and engineering; to know the manufacturer and its competitors; to know the history of the program; to know who in Congress is interested; to know the funding, the expected truck capabilities and the production schedule, etc. To know all this, your civil servant has to work closely with his peers in the Army.

His Army counterparts are going to be cooperative as long as everything is going well. But what will be their reaction when the inevitable problem occurs in the program? Developing, building and operating leading edge equipment always exposes new problems. (*This is often a surprise to the organization for reasons beyond the scope of this book. Please just accept this as a fact, so I can proceed.*) Assume the example program has a particular problem and that the Secretary of Defense doesn't think the Army is resolving the issue rapidly enough. What if the trucks have a flaw, and the delivery schedule is going to be delayed, putting several hundred millions of the Army's money at risk?

What do I mean by risk? *Any delay in a program places money at risk, because Congress only funds a program according to a proposed schedule. If the truck (in this instance) is behind schedule, then the Defense comptroller gets a say in where that money is to be alternatively used or whether it should be returned back to Congress. The Secretary of Defense always has needs for more money, and that use may not be in the Army. From the Army's perspective, a delay in the truck program not only means its requirements are not being met but also carries with it a significant chance of an additional penalty — a loss of money from the Army coffers. Naturally, the civil servants in the Army, as well as the Army military officers, are never in favor of losing money.*

When this inevitable problem occurs, without political appointee assistance, the Defense civil servant is at risk. If the civil servant has been put in the position of deciding what the Army should do differently (and consequently who in the Army has failed to put forth best effort), the civil servants in the Army are going to remember this as disloyalty long after the current Administration has departed. The civil servant is no longer going to be able to get information he needs from the Army or their contractors.

He will be unable to do his job for subsequent administrations. Future administrations will only be interested in the civil servant's performance for them—the historical reason why will not be their concern. The career civil servant in the middle of all this is destined to be **not** compensated and **not** promoted.

Most career civil servants understand these dynamics and, while they may dutifully report their thoughts, findings and recommendations in private to you, they will be understandably uncomfortable in taking the lead in confronting another part of the Department or Agency.

One of the peculiarities of Government, where you are operating without the correcting influences of the bottom line and quarterly earnings reports, is that quick corrective action usually requires a political appointee to take the lead in developing the recommendations for corrections and change. Your career civil servants will give you all the staff support you need to do so. In turn, you need to take the point.

It is also worth reemphasizing that you are also temporary help. The truck review you led may well have identified the root causes of the problem and come up with the right corrective action. However, you will be gone and the Army truck program problems will continue, unless, during the review and after, you convince the non-political part of the Army that the recommended corrective action is both proper and necessary. This requires consultation prior, during and after the review. "The Army" is a stakeholder. Consultation is essential; as it is to everything else you will do in Washington.

Abandonment

Later we are going to discuss, as a case study, an effort many of us made to reform America's export control policy. The work done to enforce the applicable legislation and regulations is done by career civil servants, and they are the experts in the nuance, history and interpretation of that policy. Remember, they are the Department's institutional memory.

In this particular instance, the contretemps involved many other Government Agencies, the Congress and the Defense Industry, which includes its own special interest groups. I was very vocal and aggressive in my personal efforts to change a decades-old policy and we were successful in unearthing this particular mossy rock from its resting place in the shade, and starting it up the hill. However, while I acted as point, I failed spectacularly to adequately protect the career civil servants who assisted me. I used their knowledge properly, but I also gave them recognition in speeches, and took them with me to the Hill and elsewhere, so they could (in my opinion) receive the proper credit and the psychic rewards of being in the know and a part of the process.

This was a serious leadership mistake

It was inadvertent, but a mistake, nevertheless, and all mistakes get recorded in Washington's box scores. Recognition of subordinates is a leadership style that is appropriate for business and the military. In both those arenas, the leader is going to be around to protect "his" people from subsequent retaliatory attacks until they acquire status and power of their own. Government is different. The political appointee will not to be there long, and civil servants don't acquire the right kind of "power." When the Administration changes, as it will, the career civil servants will still be there, and will continue to serve, or not, at the pleasure of the new political leaders.

In this case, when the new administration arrived, all of the civil servants who had served me were reassigned to less responsible positions or forced to leave their careers in Government. It was devastating to them. It affected their careers, their families and their dreams. It was my fault.

Leadership Rules

1. Career civil servants are the management and memory of the Department. Those who make it to the top are usually extremely well-qualified.
2. Expect loyalty from your career civil servants. You have all

the management tools in the bag to make this happen.
3. Career civil servants are both the worker bees and the middle management. However, <u>you</u> must lead any controversial efforts, or their future effectiveness will be compromised.

Chapter Seven

A CASE STUDY – TRUCKS

This case study focuses not only on the effective use of civil servants, but also on the difficulty of introducing change into the entrenched organizations you will find in Washington. The following study illustrates four leadership and management precepts:

- *When there is something very important to accomplish, a good way to ensure you and your staff are adequately engaged is to deliberately position yourself in the line of fire.*
- *To work effectively in any Department or Agency, you must understand the cultures of the career organizations. In Defense, the origin of this study, you must learn the cultures of the Services.*
- *Accomplishments can be realized by either working with or by changing the organization(s). Neither is easy. In Defense, each Service, as well as the Office of the Secretary of Defense, is organized differently, and disparate parts may not mesh cleanly. Again, learning is required. Change is, of course, difficult anywhere.*
- *Problems don't stay solved without follow-up.*

The Army moves by truck. Army trucks are not anything like the one your neighbor drives. Army trucks, driven by eighteen-year-olds, can motor smoothly through swamp, desert, rocks and roads, pulling tons of ammunition, up and down extraordinary inclines. America's Army requires tens of thousands of these trucks, costing several billion dollars.

The problem

While the military keeps equipment around much longer than you or I (thirty years average per truck), some time ago it was obvious to all that the Army needed replacements. The high repair costs to keep the old vehicles running was becoming a significant expense. So a new and improved design was chosen, a contract was let, a manufacturer got to work, and new trucks began rolling off the line and out to the troops. Unfortunately, there was a problem.

With no warning, while driving on straight smooth highways, two different trucks had suddenly rolled over on their sides. Actually, the trucks did not "roll," but abruptly fell onto their sides. Fortunately, no one was hurt. The press reported the first event as a rolling problem. The term, however accurate, stuck.

After the first roll over, the Army leadership told the Secretary of Defense that the problem was being addressed. The Secretary's staff relayed that information to the Press and the Congress. Nothing further was heard from the Army. When a second incident occurred a few months later, the Secretary of Defense felt he had been misled. He assigned a political appointee to investigate.

When the political appointee arrived at the truck factory, he was met by an Army Lieutenant Colonel. After some financial and technical briefings, it became obvious that the manufacturer had a good idea as to what was causing the problem, and had already developed three possible fixes, one of which was relatively inexpensive.

The Situation

There were several factors in play which influenced subsequent events:

- The cost of developing the truck had been significantly underestimated by the Army and the developer at the beginning of the program.
- The Army was not satisfied with the manufacturer. Since the costs of development had been higher that estimated, the Army had for years needed to set aside extra, unexpected, funds to complete the development. In addition, truck production was behind schedule, and each month the old trucks were in the field meant higher maintenance bills for the Army. The additional costs had not been budgeted in the annual Army appropriation, and thus dollars to repair trucks were being siphoned off from other important Army programs.
- The Army was considering suing the manufacturer to recover the extra maintenance costs on the old trucks. The Army had also notified the manufacturer that he would be expected to bear any necessary repair costs to the new trucks to correct whatever had caused them to "roll" ... (no, the Army officer who wrote that letter had not consulted his attorney as to what the signed contreact actually said, nor did he think through whether it was more important to get the right "fix," or just the cheapest one.)
- The manufacturer had lost money for several years, both in developing and manufacturing the truck. The larger parent company had demanded better quarterly results from its subsidiary or heads would roll (and they did).
- The truck had passed the Army specified testing. In tests, the truck had been driven in demanding terrain, through the swamp, around the rocks and over sixty degree hills for more than 5000 miles. The test data showed the truck would operate for the specified time between visits to the repair shop, while operating 80% of the time over unimproved terrain such as dirt roads, swamp, fields and hills.

While it would take several years to get either ready, there were two other companies which could manufacture such a truck. One of these other manufacturers was already at work developing a similar, but possibly more expensive, truck for the Marine Corps. A third bidder on the original contract had gone out of business only after losing the competition.

- When the manufacturer found an acceptable technical fix, the Army had specified that the first of the new trucks to be repaired were those overseas and those in an honor guard unit in Washington. After that, trucks were to be repaired based on mileage, the older ones first. (It would be much more cost effective to fix all the trucks on a particular post at the same time.)
- For safety reasons, the Army limited the speed the trucks were allowed to be driven until the problem could be fixed.

So, what do we have?

For starters, intense Congressional interest — not only due to concern for the soldiers driving and riding in the trucks, but also because the added Army maintenance costs were impacting the funding of other Army programs which were of special interest to Members and their constituents. In addition, the other two manufacturers capable of producing the truck were actively lobbying Congress to terminate the contract. With the possibility of two new localities in the United States gaining jobs and millions of dollars in income if the current manufacturer failed, this alternative had its own advocates in Congress.

Concurrently, the program was itself a major irritant. Since the development costs had been originally underestimated, every new year the Army had to request more funds, stating, "We have solved 'the problem.' Just give us this more money." This had gone on for years. Several people in Congress had lost patience with this story. There obviously were still problems.

Press interest? Of course. With a losing bidder going out of business, and subsequent program overruns year after year, there had been truck stories in the Defense trade press for years. When a second "roll over" occurred, some months after the Defense press representatives had assured everyone there was no systemic problem, everyone's interest was piqued. Once the Army (properly) limited the speed of the remaining new trucks, the **Army Truck Problem!** hit the front pages of the national press. Army interest? You would think so, wouldn't you? They needed tens of thousands of trucks as soon as possible. They were losing money every day maintaining their ancient fleet. The Army didn't want to wait for the Marine Corps truck to be available. Leaving Service pride aside, even if it were available, the Army didn't believe they could afford the Marine Corps truck.

So, if the Army was so interested, why was a Lieutenant Colonel (a relatively junior officer) the only military presence on scene when the Secretary of Defense sent a senior political to investigate? Why wasn't the Army sparing no effort to help that officer, and the manufacturer, fix the problem? Where were the Generals? To answer these questions, you have to understand something about the culture and particular organization of the Army.

Different organizations have different cultures, and those cultures may make solutions difficult. In all the military services, warriors have a higher status than the officers who perform in support roles. The process of acquiring anything, such as a truck, is considered a support (acquisition) job.

In the acquisition world, it is also a higher status to be involved in developing or building something that "projects force," which is code for military equipment which is designed to kill people. Consequently, while the truck program was the most <u>expensive</u> acquisition program in the Army, senior army officer supervision was focused more on their helicopter, tank and gun programs, whether or not they had equivalent technical and political problems.

There is also an inherent weakness in the manner in which the Army had organized its technical people. In the Army, the military officers and career civil servants actually managing the Army's interest in a program (the Lieutenant Colonel and his chain of command, in this instance) reported to a political appointee in the Army, who in turn answered, on acquisition matters, to an Undersecretary of Defense.

However, the bulk of the career civil servant engineering and technical competence in the Army reports to someone else. To be specific, to the Army Material Command, led by a Four Star General (the highest rank in the Army), has the Army engineering responsibility. That general reports, not to the political appointee, but rather to the Vice Chief of Staff of the Army. Thus, these two chains of command and responsibility do not intersect until they get to the Deputy Secretary of Defense, which means, for all practical purposes, the Army management and engineering chains never meet.

The following organization sketch is illustrative of the problem:

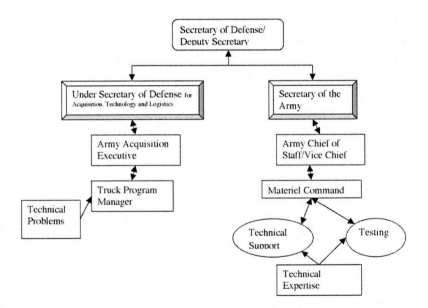

As a result of this organization, the Lieutenant Colonel, who was an excellent officer, could not get engineering assistance in his billion dollar program by simply picking up the telephone and asking. For him to get the technical help he needed, he had to press his unusual request through eight or more levels of authority. As you might expect, although he recognized he was in trouble, and had filed the proper reports, he wasn't getting much assistance.

The Army testing command also was not terribly supportive. They were the ones who had specified how the truck was to be tested and subsequently performed the testing. The trucks had rolled over after the testing command had certified they were okay. Were the testers now frantically reviewing their records to see if they had missed anything? Were they evaluating if the testing they had specified was adequate? Had they pulled any trucks back and begun testing them for more than 5000 miles, since only testing the trucks 5000 miles obviously missed some problem? Did they have representatives at the manufacturer, asking questions, looking and poking? No. No. No. No. Why not? Was it because they also reported to the engineering, not the management, chain of command?

We will skip some of the subsequent events because they are tedious. But, suffice it to say that the manufacturer, not surprisingly, settled on the cheaper fix to limit his over budget costs. That cheap fix proved unreliable, and predictably, all parties settled into a pose of financial finger pointing. However, the fact remained that the Army still needed trucks.

The Solution

Finally, a political appointee, assigned to the problem by the Secretary of Defense, became engaged in finding a solution. After consulting his career civil servants on technical, procurement contract and legal matters, he used his authority to cancel the Army truck contracts. Now, the Army's budget money was at immediate risk. This finally drove the Army's two disparate chains of command into cooperating.

Once the command attention and organization problems were resolved, many Army officers and Army career civil servants performed extraordinarily well. Within weeks, a proper fix had been designed, evaluated, installed and was being thoughtfully tested in a new regime. Subsequently, all of the trucks in the field were repaired ahead of schedule, and new, improved trucks, began rolling off the manufacturer's production line at higher quality and ever decreasing costs. What fixed this problem? First of all, the role (and attention) of the Secretary of Defense was critical. He placed the power of his office behind getting this unsatisfactory situation resolved. Defense is a large organization. There are always problems. Recognizing which problems need extraordinary actions to correct is good management. Making it happen is leadership. The Secretary had both.

Second, he assigned a political appointee who knew how to work with the career civil servants and use their expertise while, at the same time, taking personal responsibility for their recommendations. He knew that the civil servants advising him had to be shielded or they wouldn't be around to help solve the next problem. The political appointee essentially bureaucratically painted a bull's eye on his own chest, saying, "I am responsible for the truck problem."

The political appointee was not an expert on trucks or things Army. He did not know, on his first trip to the manufacturer, what the problem was, why it had occurred, or what was going to have to be done. He had never even driven a truck. But he did have some very competent civil servants by his side. By his sixth visit to the manufacturer, the testing site and the intermediate commands in the chains, he still didn't know nearly as much as the very competent Army officers and career civil servants with responsibility for the truck program. But, on the other hand, it was obvious to all that he was involved, and <u>wouldn't go away</u>, until all the right Army people were working together toward success.

The trucks have proved to be more reliable and capable than advertised. Recently, I noticed in the paper that the Army had just placed a several hundred million dollar order for more of them.

Management Rules

1. Recognize when a problem needs your personal, political, skills.
2. Learn the culture and organization of your Department/ Agency. When problems arise which defy easy solution, the culture or the organizational structure is probably throwing sand in the gears.
3. I have never met anyone who completely understood a problem from the moment he/she walked into the room. If an issue is important, learning is necessary and follow-up essential.
4. Be a big boy (or girl). Take responsibility. Shield your career civil servants from political, organizational and cultural wars. These conflicts are not their responsibility.

Leadership Rules

1. If a problem is so acute that it is of the highest priority to be fixed, then placing yourself directly in the line of fire is a wonderful device to focus your attention and efforts.
2. Nothing works well without leadership.

Chapter Eight

CONGRESS

As soon as you are comfortable with the basics of your role in your Department or Agency, it is not too soon to turn your attention, just as would any thirteenth century warrior, to the people who occupy the highest hill in town – the Congress.

Every one of you already has some contacts in Congress. As soon as you are sworn in, begin to use every opportunity to make more. It is always helpful to know someone socially, or have worked together in non-adversarial conditions, before you have to sit down on opposite sides of the table to snarl over an issue. And those days will inevitably come.

Each Department has key Senators, Representatives and staffers to whom you must be attentive. Of course, there are those Members on "your" committees. In addition, you are very interested in the thoughts and actions of those individuals on the House and Senate Appropriations and Authorization Committees and subcommittees. For specific issues you may well deal with other committees such as Government Affairs, Small Business, etc. A good starting premise is that there is no Member of Congress or staffer who can safely be ignored.

Preparation

Before you initiate contact, ensure you talk to the Congressional Relations' or Comptrollers' Offices (the latter deals with the Appropriations Committees). They will know more than you can imagine about the players. You do not want to leave your future success to luck. *I once did not do my homework before I went for lunch with a Congressman's chief of staff. When I got to the Congressman's office, the chief of staff, turned to another woman, who was casually attired in jeans and running the Xerox machine, and asked if the latter also wanted to join us. The three of us proceeded to lunch, at which I subtly, so I thought, pitched some ideas I hoped the chief of staff would support the concepts with her boss. Except for polite comments, and asking her to pass the ketchup, I essentially ignored the Xerox lady.*

The next day the Congressman called me, saying, "Dave, my wife liked your ideas, and since we have been married for thirty years, and she has managed all my campaigns, I trust her judgment more than anyone. When can you come over to personally talk?" The "Xerox woman" had kept both her maiden name and a low profile. (Although now that I thought back, she had said some things not entirely complementary to the Congressman and invited me to join her side — which I had politely declined.) I had dodged a bullet I hadn't even heard fired!

Many deadly weapons on the Hill are equipped with silencers.

Constituent Issues

Our Senators and Representatives get elected by various means, but they **stay** in office by dedicated servicing of constituent issues. When you are not responsive to a concern about a constituent issue, you are threatening a Senator's or Representative's "core capability." Let's assume you already took the earlier caution about attentiveness to Congressional correspondence seriously, and are never, ever, in the situation of starting out in the deep, dark hole of being late and inattentive to a Congressional letter. Most letters are straightforward requests for information – such as who is the proper person in the Government to contact on an issue? Other letters simply ask the Department to reply to a constituent (with a copy to the Congressman). Of the rest, in my experience, a surprisingly significant percentage of the constituent complaints which cross your desk will identify a problem in your organization you may well want to address.

Often the problem is not precisely the one the constituent has identified. For example, the constituent may complain that he "unfairly" lost a contract, and there may be very good and relevant reasons he did not win. But, concurrently, the letter may identify for you, if you think about it, a short coming which still needs attention.

In the example I am thinking of, the required debriefing the constituent received as to why he lost was either unclear, or too vague for the constituent to realize he had to correct a basic flaw before again competing for a Government contract. He could not win until he revamped his company. Since the bidder hadn't "broken the code," and kept losing, he thought the people doing the evaluation were crooked. They were not; but they also were not good communicators.

Good Government includes not giving losing contractors any reason to conjecture that the "fix" is in. (As they will from non-specific explanations as to why they lost). Good Government flourishes in an environment of open competition. In this case, we retrained the contract award debriefers and I personally met the losing contractor and wrote out for him what he had to modify in his company in order to become an acceptable Government bidder.

Returning to routine Congressional correspondence, for each response that crosses your desk for your or your boss's signature, take an extra moment to read and think carefully about tone, accuracy, resolution and permanency.

Tone. Does the letter take an indirect swipe at the Member or constituent for wasting your Department's time? You will be surprised how many drafts will do so. Remember the initial response was probably drafted by the individual in the Department whom the constituent is directly or indirectly taking to task, and no one likes criticism, especially if there is a kernel of truth involved. You may well be the first person, senior to the drafter, who even knows a Member of Congress, much less appreciates their role with respect to your Department.

Accuracy. Do you believe the response? Every now and then a response will just not quite meet your common sense test. If some bell is dinging faintly in the back of your mind, don't sign or initial the letter before you determine if the ringing is a false alarm or the fire bell.

Resolution. Does the letter do something positive to resolve the situation? Is the letter going to be of any help to the Member in responding to his constituent? If it doesn't promise something, why not? If it does, can you deliver on the commitment?

Permanency. Records live forever. You will encounter letters you have signed, many which you no longer recall, at many a witness table on the Hill. The missive will be produced, accompanied by Congressional drama and flourishes, and described as impugning your last answer. *This event will always cause an instant knot in your stomach until you have quickly reread the letter and recalled the real issue and circumstances. Now all you have to do is explain it. . .*

Ensure anything you sign, especially a letter to a Member, is going to withstand the test of time and testimony.

One in about a hundred letters is going to be terribly difficult. The most common example is one in which you believe the answer is accurate, complete, correct and right! Unfortunately, you also know in your heart this answer is not going to be acceptable to the Senator or Representative since he/she has already gone public on what he expects the Department to do.

I recommend you not sign those letters without first personally discussing the issue with the Member. There seldom is an upside to publicly embarrassing a Member of Congress for something which may have been written and auto penned by a staffer. *Sometimes a particular Member and I agreed that he would forget his query, and I would lose my answer. When I left office, I shredded a dozen letters, representing weeks of staff work, written in blood and stained in sweat, but never signed.*

In spite of all your good efforts, the world is not always fair, and sometimes an issue can not be resolved to everyone's satisfaction. In that case, the Member needs to know you have tried (with a personal review, an investigation, a study, etc.), even if he will remain unsatisfied or angry at the conclusion.

Constituent interests are important to Members, as I keep repeating, but also remember our elected representatives are intelligent men and women, even if they may not be as "reasonable" on constituent interests as you would prefer. I settled some very hard issues by going the extra mile to explore alternatives, and bending over backwards to reexamine a constituent's issues, thus giving the Member something he could deliver to his constituent. In many cases the result was not what the constituent had asked for nor what he wanted; but my extra effort demonstrated to the constituent that his Congressman/woman had tried, and established for the Member that I appropriately respected his/her office.

In a few memorable cases, the constituent was so outrageous in his continued demands he eventually tried the patience of the Member, and together, the Congressman and I crafted a plan to ensure the constituent completely sawed off the limb on which he had insisted perching. "The system," of course, took the blame.

Standing or Stake-Holding

Members have standing on issues involving their constituents, issues falling under their Committee's jurisdiction, and issues upon which they have expressed an interest.

In spite of your best efforts, frequently you are not going to be able to do what a Member or his constituent desires. As a result, events out of your control may make you the object (whether specifically identified or not) of one of his or her sound bites. If this happens, instead of uselessly retaliating, I recommend you take every opportunity to try to balance the ledger with that Senator or Congressman by making sure the Member gets credit for those times in which Lady Fortune deposits the croupier's ball in his slot on the wheel (e.g., something has happened which is going to improve the prestige or employment in his Congressional area).

The most organized Administration I observed set up strict rules for the notification of Members when someone in their district or state had been recognized or awarded a contract. The larger the contract, the more senior the person who called the Senator/Representative – some calls were made by the President. The exact time such calls can be made is subject to legal restrictions as well as informal agreements with Congress. Your Congressional Relations and Comptrollers offices will know these rules, and will make (or broker) the decisions as to who will be called first, and by whom. Don't miss an opportunity to personally deliver good news, for you are certainly going to have to deliver unpleasant political news often enough. Good tidings are a fine opening to someone you do not currently know well.

Consultation

If a Member has standing on an issue, and a proposed change in issue policy gets to the Press before the Member knows about it, he is going to consider this was done deliberately and act accordingly. I know you are busy and just forgot, and your significant other will confirm this, if only asked, but your explanation to the contrary never goes well.

Imagine the conversation:

"Congressman, I know that you are the one that decides on my Department's level of funding, and publicly supports our agenda, and I certainly appreciate how you handled that last hearing, but I didn't care enough about you to know you were interested in that issue. I am sorry you got asked that question on television last night and looked like you didn't know what was going on. That reporter was surely clever! My spouse even laughed."

"No, strike all that, let me start over. Mr. Congressman, I knew you were interested and we still need your support,

but I was busy and it was more important to go home to dinner than call you. I wanted to see how the issue played on the eleven o'clock news."

"No, no, I think I have the wrong number. uhh – uhh – uhh... This was a crank call. Goodbye, Sir."

There is another good reason for prior consultation with Members who have standing. Washington is a political town. The 535 current Members of Congress are obviously politicians of skill and currency. Even if you had years as a staffer, or even served in Congress, the current Hill residents may well have good ideas as to how a particular policy or program can best be structured and sold at this time.

Investigations

Part of the system of checks and balances in our government is Congressional oversight of the Executive Branch. Oversight often takes the form of investigations, which in turn, often lead to hearings. The General Accounting Office (or GAO) does investigations for Congress. In addition, different Committees may also have their own investigative bodies to get information or review how a decision was reached. No matter how good and impartial these people are, remember the Congress is directly paying their salaries. If a particular Member has a strong view on a subject, surprise of surprises, the investigation usually leans over backward to support that view.

You will have the opportunity to comment on these reports – but many politicals miss that chance! Make sure your people are adequately attentive. Yes, they have other work, and the investigations often drag on for months. Then suddenly, with an unforgivingly short deadline, the Department is required to comment. The subsequent deadline can easily be missed. If you do miss a due date, you later are going to have to stand up some place in public and explain, why, if the report was so flawed, you didn't even comment when the Department had the opportunity?

Unless instructed, your people may not recognize the danger

of letting the error in a record go uncorrected, or the need to include a statement of the Defense position to ameliorate a critical report. Unless you give them clear guidance, they may not even tell you an investigation is underway.

Don't let any investigation go unread or uncommented upon, and be alert to inform your bosses of investigations which are going astray or have the potential to be embarrassing to the Department or Administration. To solve all of these problems, I assigned one very senior and capable career civil servant as the contact point for all investigations in my area. She was the only person an outside investigator could speak to in order to start a review. She knew when each was initiated, kept me informed, coordinated comments within the Department, ensured I saw each report, and that I concurred with our comments (or lack thereof) before they were mailed.

Legislation

Congress passes new laws every single year, often at the request of the Administration. In preparation, your Department/Agency/Service will be asked to organize a legislative package of items the Administration will submit. Consultation with those Industry groups interested in your particular sector is always worth considering as the process evolves. This resulting package will subsequently be vetting at every level up to the White House. In most Departments these items must pass through the General Counsel and Deputy's office at the Office of the Secretary before being addressed to the Old Executive Office Building.

Your staff will draft a list of suggested legislation. You should expect them to often be passionate about some items — no matter how politically impossible or potentially disastrous the legislation. But no matter how much your staff believes, and pants for your approval, you need to review each item very carefully. Be alert, for the same items may have been submitted by the Department bureaucracy for years. If you once again send the same issues forward, without knowing the context and laying the appropriate spadework, the Congressional staffers (the same ones you need to continually impress with your professionalism), will think you are naïve – at best.

You also want to make sure a new law won't be worse than the alternative. A good thumb rule is that legislation which deletes previous legislation is probably okay, but anything else calls for a great deal of thought. You need to make sure you have evaluated all the unintended consequences of any new law. Remember that it is much, much easier to get a new law, even one of questionable value, passed by Congress, than it is to get a law changed or repealed – even one that is widely acknowledged to be "bad" law. On the other hand, the Administration controls the implementing regulations, and regulatory change is frequently all that is needed to fix a "bad" law. In most cases, you don't need Congressional action, just a little backbone.

Many staff proposals for new laws are simply a reflection of a lack of ability or will to do the coordination necessary to achieve consensus within the Administration in order to alter the regulations. A proposed new law may also be an attempt by one Agency to use the Congress to change the behavior of another Agency. Either conduct is similar to that of the teenager who can't be bothered with checking the pressure in his car's tires, but then asks for a new auto because the "springs seem bad."

The quicksand of new legislation. It is also easy to personally become prey to "new legislation" quicksand. Imagine this situation. You are on the Hill, talking for the first time to the Chairman of the subcommittee that deals with your particular issue, and you have found the Chairman is bright, considerate and philosophically right in step with your own beliefs on environment, research and development, small business, whatever. And he says, "I would be happy to sponsor whatever legislation you might need to do your job better." You perk up. In the job for only three months, and already I am being asked to help make the laws! How nice, he realizes how bright and dedicated I am.

The Chairman continues, "Why don't you just pass your ideas to Alice, here, within the next two weeks, and we'll get going on rounding up my colleagues?"

Upon your return to the Department, you locate the staffer who is familiar with writing draft legislation, and he says, "No sweat, I can do that this week."

Later, you happen to mention this to your boss, and she gives you a cold eye and asks you to talk to the General Counsel, who informs you of the detailed bureaucratic process for submitting legislative changes.

"No way, just routing to all those offices will take three months," you think to yourself, "and my staff says Commerce (or Justice or State or _____ {fill in the blank}) is part of the problem and will never agree."

You leave the meeting thinking, "Perhaps I will just pass my draft over to the Committee in an unmarked envelope."

Don't do it!

You were unknowingly already up to your ankles in muck when you departed the Chairman's office. When you left, his staff was probably already pinning your picture up on their "victims" board. Think carefully. You are charged with doing the best job for your Department and the Administration in your area. How can you be so sure you alone know all of the Administration's interests? American Government is complicated.

The basic rule is – unless you have truly considered all the ramifications, you can probably get along just fine without new legislation.

Let me tell you how an "innocent" piece of legislation once ruined my day.

Several of us had been working an issue in which our Secretary was personally interested. He wanted a change in Administration policy on a sensitive issue with another country. We needed to establish a proposed agreement within the Administration. State would then negotiate the final wording with the other Nation.

After six months, we finally gave up on inter-Agency coordination, because we had gotten as much agreement as there was to get. Then the unresolved issue moved up to the White House. After several emotional meetings, the President stepped in and brought all the Cabinet members into line.

As soon as the Press got wind of some disagreement within the Administration, they began poking around. Immediately, the Congress was interested. The proposed agreement was specifically not constructed as a new treaty, to avoid the need for Senate approval. Some in the Senate viewed this aspect rather dimly. They voiced their concern. In reply, we said the negotiation was part of the normal course of business between Nations, and fell well under existing laws.

You may well wonder if someone in the Administration, perhaps in the Agencies the President had "to convince," was "leaking" to Congress? That is certainly a possibility. Each Department's Committees believe they are the only people in Washington with the right to beat up on their Department. At the same time, these Committees frequently view "their" Agency as "their" voice in the Administration. When one Department or Agency is rolled, their Committee usually doesn't have to be asked twice before they volunteer to step in to limit the bureaucratic damage to "their" boy. Frequently, their efforts involve passing a law which limits the Executive's power. This is definitely not in any President's best interests.

The interested Senators finally, and reluctantly, agreed with what we were proposing, but remained concerned that we might go "too far" during negotiations. They thus suggested passing a law to put in black and white what we were all thinking about. I made a mistake — I agreed.

Having decided to go along with a law, we did our best to look out for "unintended consequences." I read and reread suggested language. Our Congressional specialists reviewed it. All the General Counsel's offices in all the Departments and Agencies read the proposed language. We agreed there were several issues which were important, and others which were simply bargaining chips to fall during the negotiations with the other Nation. We carefully used "shall" to identify those things we had to have, and "should" to precede those items which were to be left to the negotiation. In order to speed the process and get consensus within the Administration, I agreed to let in some worthless "should" items.

Congress passed the law exactly as we wrote it. State started the negotiations.

Shortly thereafter, the General Counsel in one of the key Departments (one the President had rolled to start with) returned to private practice. Before the negotiations with the other Nation could be completed, his relief wrote an opinion stating that, for the purpose used, each place the law stated "shall" or "should," must always be read as meaning "shall."

This interpretation made continued negotiations almost impossible.

Two years of work wasted. The Secretary's desires thwarted. The President's intent unexecuted. I never did get the new law revised.

You understand current laws — frequently you and your staff have had years to fully understand their consequences and effects. Beware of the unintended effects of what you might get with new legislation. It may take several years of effort, and a great many of the solid gold trading coins you possess, to get a bad law "fixed" — if you ever do.

Leadership Rules

1. Congress has the money for, and ultimate approval of, everything your Department needs. Pay the same attention to Congress as you would in your old hometown to the mayor, the sheriff, the editor of the newspaper, the feed store owner and the banker who holds the mortgage on the homestead —all rolled into one.
2. Recognize that constituent interests inevitably require great care in resolving.
3. Never sign a letter, especially a reply to a Member of Congress, without carefully considering both the explicit and implicit questions it may raise.
4. Consult. If you do **not** intend to do prior consultation with a Member on an issue on which he has standing, do so with all due deliberation.
5. Ensure you are attentive to Congressional investigations.
6. Be very careful when you request a new law from Congress. You may well get what you ask.

Chapter Nine

YOUR VALUE ADDED

You've done what was necessary to get the appointment confirmed, established both yourself and your office, started making new friends about town and are hard at work. Now is perhaps the time to reflect a bit – just what is the value added by a political appointee?

Your value added is partly a result of the experience and knowledge you bring to the table of national issues. The professionals who run your Agency are frequently prisoners of their own milieu. They have spent their lives improving the performance of their organizations. Supported by the American people, and with funds from Congress, they have been very successful. America won the race to space, has the best military, and has the highest standard of living in the world. All of this reflects the exceptional past performance of our Government.

However, there are two very basic and un-American structural problems in each of our Government's Departments and Agencies. One is that, unlike nearly everything else in America, there is no competition. There is only one Justice, one NASA, and one

State Department in America, just as there is only one American Army. Yet, one of our fundamental tenets is that we have grown and remained strong as a direct result of the benefits of competition-driven innovation.

In the United States, when a particular company or industry has achieved near-monopoly conditions (for example, the railroads) or stayed wedded too long to old technology (e.g., the steel industry), history has been unforgiving. Our economy and Country is designed to tolerate and grow from the redistribution of capital that new ideas and technology produce, as painful as this may be in the short-term to large groups of individuals.

However, competition is not the norm in Government. We can not afford a duplicate government. Concurrently, our nation's security would not survive the eventual stultification that is the hallmark of a monopoly.

America is not going to alter our monopoly Government. It is the result of a historic compromise, between fiscal limitations on one hand (we have enough trouble affording one Government!), and, using Defense as an example, a desire to optimize our warfighting capability in the field on the second. However, as we cannot put up with the "natural" economic results that would flow from a business monopoly, America cannot tolerate the negative consequences of the socialistic organization of our Government. We must have powerful forces working to balance that necessary construction. One of your important tasks is to prevent this inherent flaw from overheating and cracking the American melting pot.

The second basic structural problem with Government Agencies is that each is centrally controlled, organized and operated, just as were the socialistic countries, which have fallen like dominoes over the past forty years. A centrally controlled organization can make the trains run on time. It can put effective military forces in the field.

Unfortunately, as socialistic governments have proven again and again, central control stifles initiative, innovation and the redirection of resources to new breakthrough ideas and technologies. As a result, while this would not be true in American business, a senior career civilian or military leader, who does not recognize the importance of a particular innovation, whether it be an economic idea, or revolutionary military weapon, can thwart the new concept from flowering.

Each Department needs "outside" influence to encourage or force change. Left completely to themselves, the careerists in a Bureau are frequently very comfortable with the organizational structure that exists, the ideas and technologies it has embraced and those tactics it has practiced. But in many areas, our free-enterprise-commercial America advances much faster than our Government. In the last decade alone, one can observe significant "civilian" leap forwards in many areas, including sensors, communications, computing capability, transportation, gender discrimination and the use of remotely operated vehicles. Unfortunately, and perhaps inherently, government is different. As a result, each Department frequently needs the introduction of new ideas from non-traditional sources.

You, by design and the President's appointment, are one of those "outside" forces. People will seek you out to advocate systems, tactics and policies not currently accepted. These individuals may be right, or, alternatively, dead wrong. You will be expected to judge, as well as to ensure something "new" isn't automatically labeled "bad."

While you are making a judgment, be sure you do not succumb to the (too human) impulse to label the careerists, who tend to support the status quo, as "obstacles." Part of the goal of this book is to help you avoid this by pointing out: what the careerist groups are particularly well qualified to accomplish; where their training and their culture may hinder them; and where you will have to take a leadership role. Many political appointees make the mistake of "throwing out the dog with the bathwater," and completely ignore the professionals. You will learn better over time, but frequently only after precious and irreplaceable months or even years have passed, and errors have been made—unnecessarily hindering future progress. The loss of time and the needless missteps are both completely avoidable.

This is a point which deserves mentally underlining. Many Secretaries, both Republican and Democrat, experience their first setback in office as a direct result of a lack of understanding, and consequently a lack of trust, of the careerists, be they civil servants, professionals or military officers. A political appointee never has to agree with a recommendation from these quarters, but you are sailing into professional danger if you exclude them from your councils and/or appear to not even deign to listen to their opinions and judgments.

Given that you are going to establish the appropriate professional relationships within your Department, Agency or Bureau, let's now talk about the contacts outside the Department that will be important to you. There are several groups to which you need be attentive. The most influential ones are the President and his Administration, the Congress, and the "Industry" (including the "think tanks" and special interest organizations, such as the unions). A peripheral impact group is the Press.

White House

Your most important support in the Administration will come from the White House. Depending on the seniority of your position, as well as your pre-existing networks of friendships in and around the White House, you will have natural contact points in the White House or the Old and New Executive Office Buildings. Even with the best of networks, you should use every opportunity to establish new personal contacts and renew old acquaintances.

Your budget and administrative policies either originate in or are evaluated and coordinated with the rest of the Administration and approved by the President's team in the Office of Management and Budget. In addition, many of the issues you will be involved with day-to-day will be worked through the National Security Council, the Domestic Policy Council or other White House organization. Events will force the Department to dip oars in many troubled waters. Tough problems are eventually resolved by or through the good offices of these fellow political appointees. It is important they get to know you and recognize the added value you bring to the table. Each White House contact will someday prove useful.

Congress

The Congress has several roles. As we have already pointed out, they have the (your) money. If everything the public desired Government to provide were funded, our tax money would be spent many times over. The President proposes a distribution, and the Congress is the final arbiter. Therefore, you will spend a great deal of time convincing Congress and its staff both of the value and the need for your programs, funded as recommended in the President's and the Department's Budget request.

This communication with Congress is where you are going to be expected to provide much of the political-appointee-value-added. Unlike the military, as we will discuss later, you don't wear a particular uniform. You wear the suit of a political appointee. You are definitively part of the President's and the Secretary's Team. You are also part of the Democratic Team or the Republican Team. You may be a part of other teams which have a cachet in cross-cutting groups in Congress, such as the Union Team, the California Team, or the Minority Team. Humans naturally group together to get things done. Membership in all these teams is useful in establishing initial relationships with Congress.

Many in the Congress have an individual philosophy as to how your department should operate, as well as detailed knowledge of particular programs, based on their years in public office and their personal attention to areas they believe especially important. Their interest in these areas is often based solely on principle, rather than politics. When this is so, they have the augmented power of the righteous, whether or not the Administration believes they are correct in general or specific.

In decisions which significantly change the thrust of programs in their areas of expertise, Congressmen must be consulted, briefed, and made partners to the Department. Otherwise, you will be stopped. It is senseless to initiate a fight which can be avoided, so prior consultation is a must. Even if you know you cannot convince the Congressman, he or she still must be consulted, or you will be halted out of general courtesy or on procedural grounds.

Another reason Congress is very interested in the Department is because decisions you propose to make will affect their constituencies. This is most obvious in Defense. A new weapons program will add jobs in some areas, and the program it nudged out of the budget will result in unemployment in other neighborhoods. Be prepared. Nearly all the decisions in which you are involved will involve some political controversy. Decisions to change the way health care is provided have job ramifications, just as does a decision not to pursue a specific technology. In fact, decisions to move any specific program at less than breakneck speed mean less money spent in some State or landing in the billfold of someone who not only believes his alternative is correct, but can inevitably get the ear of at least one Senator or Representative.

Reorganization of responsibilities, troops, or capability also affects communities and their voters. Since these decisions are the essence of the budget you have produced, and large sums of money are involved, Congress is interested. Particular Members will have a constituent interest in these issues. That constituent interest is always important, but even more so if the Senator or House Member has a seat on one of your Committees.

Congressmen who are perfectly rational when discussing issues of principle, can frequently be much more emotional and demanding when considering constituent issues. They have to be: they represent those constituents.

No matter what level political appointee you are, you are going to get to meet a lot of Senators, Representatives and their staffers.

The Industry

As a political appointee, you are the entry point for all the outside organizations seeking to influence government decisions. I will term all of these the "Industry," but understand that my definition is very inclusive. I include those companies that make products your Department uses or regulates; groups which represent the careerists on compensation, health and retirement issues: civilian employee unions: think tanks and those individual Americans who consider, comment upon and try to influence Departmental policies and decisions. This is a large group. Several Departments spend a lot of money, and all Government agencies affect a lot of lives. You have to expect a lot of kibitzers.

Depending on the job you hold, one or more of these groups is going to be interested in advising and influencing you. You need to listen as much as you have time. Some of the individuals asking to be heard occupied your chair in an earlier Administration and did a fine job. Political circumstances may have changed, and time passed, but these are bright people who have much to offer.

You also can't turn up your nose at self-serving advice. In fact, most of the great ideas about systems and components which have significantly improved America came directly from a company or group of people who hoped to make a profit from a particular idea. Since new ideas result in new business, and every company is continually trying to grow, each industry is constantly generating and selling new ideas --- just as the company that is currently supporting doing the job the "old" way is dedicated to pointing out the inherent problems in the new idea and trying to kill it. It is often competition and duel by viewgraph, but it is the closest thing in Washington to the competitive atmosphere that has made our country great.

You have a portfolio to consider change. Be prepared, you are going to be a target of a large number of industry briefs.

Press

Often the press will be handled by your public affairs people, but realize that you have the pertinent official title, as well as an in-depth understanding of the issue, which the public affairs person may not be able to replicate. You have more credibility and what you say will be newsworthy. That's your added value

Since your job involves the use of all means to convince the

Congress and others of the correctness of the Administration's position, and the Congress reads the newspapers and watches television, it is going to be difficult to avoid the press. They are not called the Fourth Estate because someone could not spell press.

There is normally not a great deal of praise for the press in an Administration. Since their readers/viewers are often more titillated by miscalculations and misdeeds than in a job well done, the press feeds that interest, and this inevitably is embarrassing to some of your peers, if not yourself. Well it is a tough town, and believe it or not, the great majority of the press is interested in both good government and America. The problem is, they frequently do not understand all the aspects of an issue which lead to a particular decision or Administrative position, and they can only report what they know. So, if you want them to support a particular Administration position, the press must understand the information and considerations which are not classified. There is a role here for you and your Department's political Team.

Different administrations have different press policies. Learn your ground rules early because one day your boss is going to call you up and tell you to talk to the press. "Talking to the Press" is not something that comes naturally to most people, so, before you do, and in fact as soon as you get in office, I recommend you take the public affairs training which is available. If you came to the Administration from an advocacy position, you may already have had similar training. In spite of that advantage don't pass up the opportunity to participate. It will be a good refresher and invaluable to your success. Recording your performance on film, the training lets you observe your own performance, which is much more effective than advice and counsel.

When dealing with the press, remember these key things:
- Know your subject;
- Be truthful;
- Stay on message;
- Don't answer questions:
  When you don't know the answer:
  When it's not your bailiwick, or

When you don't want to; and
* Stay on message.
The repetition is not an accident.

Style

Political appointees must be the leaders in a fast-paced environment packed with tense moments, high stakes decision-making and unreasonable deadlines. It takes unique qualities to keep your cool and lead your team through this environment on a daily basis. It is the excitement and adrenaline high which attract so many appointees to their positions. But it also is an environment which tests each and every one of them and nakedly displays their true leadership skills.

Many political appointees are great natural leaders. The best I worked for made the staff much more effective by understanding their people were performing as well as they could. If it wasn't working, the leader was doing something wrong. Good leaders understand when a little humor or digression helps break the tension, and when an impasse can best be resolved by a good night's sleep.

An effective leader also adjusts his/her schedule to ensure he is always operating, like a fifties' Volkswagen, with a reserve tank. When you are working at the outer limit of your capacity, you can not absorb disappointment, or the necessity to rework an issue just one more (necessary) time.

That tension and frustration flow directly from your brow to your subordinates' shoulders, adding an unnecessary load to the burden they are already carrying for you. You need to be the shock absorber for the pressure that pulses into your office. A good leader cares about his people so they can take better care of him.

Most of us can be better if we simply work to avoid the common errors of poor leadership. Everyone knows that the good leader does not upbraid someone who is simply reporting an unfortunate fact or bad news. We have all heard the old saw about "Not shooting the messenger." We may know it is bad, but many political appointees still do it! Not good.

Losing your temper can have devastating consequences – both on your staff and on your reputation. Some individuals lose their temper because they don't understand the issue. A common reason is that a briefer may use too many acronyms or explain an issue too rapidly to follow. **This will happen more than once!** The people talking to you work a problem daily. This problem is their life. Few people are great communicators. Most will assume you know facts you do not, and the briefer may also be more than a little nervous in briefing someone of your stature.

Don't be afraid to ask simple questions until you get the speaker back to something you do understand, and then build from there. Don't lose your temper. It will only confuse your briefer. He may even take it personally. In either case, your loss of temper will make others reluctant to volunteer more information, which you may vitally need.

I once worked for a political appointee who had been a Hill staffer his entire career and apparently found that the loss of temper in that venue helped him get his way. It was a poor leadership trait, but he wasn't working with many other people in his staff on the Hill, and had only to keep the confidence of his boss. He had gotten by with this trait on the Hill. Unfortunately, he failed to appreciate that his move to the Pentagon was a move to a new culture and a new territory. At State and Defense, several people have been actually shot at by someone who intended them harm. A temper tantrum is significantly less frightening.

After this political appointee publicly lost his temper a couple of times, people quickly, and correctly, decided he simply didn't understand much about the Department. In the normal course of events, many would have spent extra time to explain things so that he could be a contributing member of the Team. However, because of his temper, the process was too unpleasant. Therefore, many of his staff decided the effort just wasn't worth the emotional stress. Military officers and career civil servants began to avoid his office. He soon lost his effectiveness and decided to move on – out of government.

Second to personal style, the most frequent reason for the loss of political appointee temper occurs when events are just not going your way. They frequently may not. Get used to it.

You are dealing with tough, complex, issues in a very dynamic environment. There are bright people in Washington who believe differently from you and your boss, and they may be working very hard to thwart you. Difficulty goes with the territory. If you always succeed easily, or through your first assault, maybe you are not taking on hard enough problems.

When events go awry, don't lose your temper. You are not only losing valuable thinking time, you are also inevitably frightening those around you. Your staff won't be sure if you are mad at them, or at something they failed to do. You are freezing, through fear and uncertainty, the very minds of those whom you rely upon for ideas and counsel. These are your people. You may decide to replace them, but don't reduce their effectiveness in the interim.

I am not saying that a purposeful loss of temper, even given all the bad things it does, is not useful on some occasions. The epiphany of actually seeing a quivering sword in a stone can be a useful leadership device. However, if you are using this tool more than once every three or four months, then the tool is using you.

With respect to your professional reputation, a loss of temper may say things about yourself you would rather went unsaid.

One of the very best leaders I saw in the Pentagon always managed to reach down for additional personal reserves whenever the situation required. I was in innumerable meetings with him late at night, when we had to have an answer, but were shooting blanks, and icy barbs had become the staples of conversation. Inevitably, he would choose the right moment to digress with a shaggy dog story, or a reflection on the IQ of whoever was causing our current problem,

"Shoot low boys, they're riding on Shetlands."

His timing was always impeccable. When everyone quit laughing, or criticizing his humor, somehow you could get back to thinking constructively about the problem again, rather than continuing to do a slow burn about what the person across the table had earlier implied about your sainted Mother.

He was the exceptional leader we should all should aspire to be.

Leadership Rules

1. You don't run the Department by yourself. Many Americans are very interested. You are going to be "helped" by the White House, other Departments and Agencies, the Congress, the Industry and the Press. You need to work with each one. In this process, the careerists and career civil servants in the Department or Agency are going to be valuable assets for you.
2. Political appointees introduce change into Government. Political appointees are your Agency's or Department's "market forces."
3. Political appointees represent the Department to Congress and the press. To be effective, stay on message with both.
4. Don't lose your temper and prove you don't belong.
5. Protect your people from the pressure surges that are inevitable in your office, so they can effectively think, work, and help you.

Chapter Ten

CASE STUDY –
BERETS

Since we have just talked about Congress and your Value Added, let us now do a case study which melds the two and also foreshadows our later discussion of the press, the military, hearings and testimony.

Change is difficult in a large bureaucracy, and your Department is a large bureaucracy. This case study illustrates how difficult it is to make even the smallest organizational change, as well as some of the leadership and management tools which will be essential to your success:

Know the facts better than, and before, your opponents.
Protect the career civil servants who perform well.
Practice the art of dealing with Congress.

The Situation

When a business leader wants to transform his company, he or she frequently initiates a campaign, complete with a slogan and "team" apparel. Each morning of the promotion, the janitors don hats, the blue collar workers put on T-shirts and the executives carefully pin buttons to their lapels.

When a leader of a Service wants to send a message to his hundreds of thousands of people, he also may choose to change their uniforms. It is because of past leadership campaigns that some officers in the Navy wear brown shoes while others wear black, as well as why the Air Force uniform no longer looks like that of a commercial airline pilot's. This is the story of how the Army came to wear berets.

For several years after the Cold War, there was much discussion about how well (or poorly) the Army was adapting to the post-Cold-War environment. Not all the comments were positive. After Kosovo, the new Army Chief of Staff was determined to transform the Army, and he had the Secretary of Defense's explicit blessings.

The Chief promptly initiated several dramatic changes.

First, the Chief was determined that the Army of the future would roll on the new wheels American industry was perfecting for the Sport Utility Vehicle industry. The Army currently traveled on tracks – those metal cleats that clank so loudly in war movies. Tracks had been a great technical innovation for their time. However, the Chief did not see a lot of America out buying tank treads, and they were difficult to maintain in the field. He correspondingly did not see a great deal of American industry research money going into advancing the state of the art of track construction and manufacturing.

On the other hand, the popularity of sport utility vehicles had, in only a few years, brought about dramatic advances in wheel and tire technology. The Chief was determined to leverage those advances for the Army. It was past time for the Army to take advantage of the billions of dollars of commercial investment and new technology extant in the rapidly growing business of sport utility vehicles.

He made the decision to go with tires, and held a competition for manufacturers to make the new vehicles.

Subsequently, while new manufacturers were gearing up to produce sufficient new wheeled vehicles, those individuals who had disagreed with the decision, from traditional tank tread manufacturers to old "tankers," were busy licking their wounds and looking for the opportunity to turn the clock back. Soon, an opportunity presented itself. It was an indirect approach, but it might do the trick. The opening had to do with uniforms.

Elite units in the military wear distinctive headgear, in addition to their individual Unit badges. The normal soldier at the time wore a dark green cap, something like a baseball cap, while the most widely known elite Army units wore berets. Army Rangers wore distinctive black berets, jauntily cocked over one eye

Recall how business leaders use clothes to send a message of change? The Army is America's Army, and the Chief was determined to send a message to all of America that this was a new, transformed, Army. Concurrently, he wanted to get the message across that the Army needed everyone, and no particular individual, unit or specialty was uniquely important to the success of the future Army. Everyone was important. The Army needs all skills. If pressed about this concept, he would simply say, "I was carried wounded from two battlefields. When I looked up, none of the people carrying me to safety were wearing berets."

As his method of sending both these messages of change, he decided to outfit all of America's soldiers in black berets. He directed his staff to have this accomplished by the next annual Army Birthday Ball, six months hence.

The Problem

I know it may seem crazy if you have never been in the military, but part of the lore of each Service is the history as to why each uniform piece is, and remains, precisely the way it is, from the marines "Red Stripe of Chapultepec," to the piece of cloth that still hangs down every sailor's back to protect his whites from the tar used to grease the pigtails of his eighteenth century predecessor.

The Army Rangers, especially the retired ones, were particularly not happy about the "loss" of their distinctive black beret. As Americans frequently do when they are discontented with an Administration policy, the ex-Rangers appealed to Congress, where several retired Rangers happened to be staffers. Subsequently some mumbling was heard from the Hill, but not enough to concern the Pentagon since no one on "their" Committees was too upset.

At the same time, getting everyone in berets by the Army birthday was logistically difficult. Producing enough berets to outfit the Army may seem like a minor challenge for industrial America, but that was not the case. These are special berets, especially made for military units, and intended to send a particular jaunty message. Manufacturing each was a special process. The Army normally needed about 10,000 berets a year, and the commercial industry had sized itself accordingly. Now the Army needed to buy two million in the next six months!

Military uniform berets were made by unique machines which had been discontinued in the 1930's. There were a few machines left in one area of the United States, and the rest were found in India, Indonesia, England, Canada and China. No one built the machines anymore because there was no commercial demand for military-like berets. In fact, only one company in America remained outfitted to make berets, and two million berets in six months far exceeded its production facilities. It would take the whole world's capacity to fill the Army's order.

So the career civil servants in the Defense purchasing system turned to the task. As their first assignment, they knew they were going to have to deal with the Buy American Act.

The Buy American Act requires (only) the Department of Defense to buy from American firms unless the quantity and quality can not be produced in time to meet military need. Some years earlier, to expedite meeting conflict requirements, the authority to make this decision had been passed down to the career civil servants directly involved in purchasing the equipment ordered by military commanders.

In accordance with the Buy American Act, the civil servants first awarded an order to the sole American firm for as many berets as the Company believed it could make. Then they properly waived the buy American Act to award as many berets as the qualified manufacturers in England and Canada could produce. After that, the rest of the contract was appropriately competed throughout the world.

The most reliable manufacturers turned out to be a couple of companies in China.

Now, returning to the issue of wheels for the Army, it was difficult for those who didn't believe the Army needed to be "transformed" onto wheels to argue with the Chief of Staff's professional judgment about Army vehicle tracks or treads; he was an authority on tanks and the Army. But everyone in America thinks they know something about hats!

If his critics could successfully attack his choice of headgear, it might well damage the Chief's overall credibility or at least cause him to spend so much time and political capital defending the berets that he might not have sufficient energy left to abolish tracks. The beret issue offered just the opening the Chief's opponents had been waiting for. "China! Those communistic bastards' hats on the heads of our American boys! P'shaw! (And stronger.)"

This complaint struck a responsive chord within America. An incident had just occurred with China. China was illegally retaining an American surveillance airplane (and the crew) that had been forced to land after a collision with a harassing Chinese jet. For the moment, everyone in America was looking for a way to both pressure and punish the Chinese. Suddenly the "Chinese berets" became front page news across the United States. Energized by the "track lobby," as well as current events, the House Small Business Committee called for hearings — why hadn't all the beret business been awarded to Americans?

Immediately, all legislative progress on Army transformation stopped in Washington. The public sentiment was pretty clear that the Army wasn't going to roll forward on wheels driven by American soldiers wearing Chinese berets. But, without the foreign manufactures, it would take at least four years for the only American company to make enough berets to outfit the Army. Would the

Chief be prevented from sending his message of change? Would losing the beret issue damage his authoritarian credibility and turn back the clock on his tracks/tires decision?

It wasn't only the Chief of Staff of the Army's credibility at stake, for the Secretary of Defense had heartily concurred (and quietly spurred) the decision to move from tracks to wheels. As the days moved on with the China incident unresolved, and more ex-Rangers marched to Washington to oppose black berets on everyone, it became bureaucratically evident that the Chief's decision had to be successfully defended!

Solution – Get The Facts

The first key step was ensuring that any defense of the beret "issue" was based on all the facts. Had everyone in the Government truly complied with all the laws, regulations and processes in awarding the beret contracts overseas? Had the Buy American Act been properly waived? Were all small business rules, which permit preferential set asides for American small businesses, followed?

The political appointees in the Pentagon conducted an investigation. After careful review, they determined there had been one "minor oversight." A follow-up review was performed to evaluate all similar transactions in the last five years, throughout Defense, to see if the "oversight" were truly that, or instead, a systemic problem.

As a result of the assessments, it was apparent that the career civil servants had done an exceptional job. There was no reason to cancel the procurement of the berets. Of equal importance, the Government witnesses were not going to be surprised at any Congressional hearing.

Military and Political in Step

The second step was developing a strategy that kept the senior military officers and political appointees in step with each other. It is fairly easy for Congress to exploit an issue where there is daylight between the two. On the other hand, as long as the two are truly hand-in-glove, Pentagon politicals have a real advantage. Congress is uncomfortable publicly attacking someone in uniform.

Remember, the real issue was change. The procurement issue was simply a sideshow to try to delay change until the current Chief left office. Congress would surely not confirm a next Chief unless he gave the "right" confirmation hearing answer to any question on change. "Black berets" were merely stalking horses. The senior staffer for the Government Reform Committee, who had volunteered to help the Small Business Committee, did not even disguise this charade at the hearing pre-meetings. He started out very calmly,

"We appreciate you coming over to talk about the hearings. I was a Ranger, but now I am an attorney, and I am only interested in whether or not you legally purchased those black berets."

But he couldn't contain himself any further. His face actually mottled and he leaned across the table and snarled, "I earned my beret, it was not <u>given</u> to me by some Chief!" Well, we had established the tiger had spots.

The Army and Secretary of Defense's united position was established after some internal negotiation (few strong men start out completely in agreement). The Secretary and the Chief both became comfortable with the concept of segregating and storing the Chinese-manufactured berets, and proceeding to issue troops the berets made elsewhere. This served the dual purpose of simultaneously sending a message to China that international conduct could affect their international trade, while still providing the Army sufficient berets to have most troops wearing them for the celebration of the birthday. Delivery of the final shipment would be close, but it could be done.

The final obstacle was the Congressional hearing. The hearing would be live on CNN and subsequently rebroadcast several times that week. The ongoing flap with China ensured that each Committee Member would get an unusual amount of air time. The Congressmen were going to do their very best to look good for their constituents. Some may have even secretly looked to impress a wider audience. Didn't Richard Nixon rise to fame from some hearings with the Army over Communists?

The Committee gave it their best shot. They lined up the best witnesses they could find. They had an ex-Ranger who marched a thousand miles to deliver a petition to Congress from other ex-Rangers who had also "earned" their berets. They had an attractivesmall business owner who maintained she could have made the berets; if only she had been given a chance (the Army had previously evaluated her product and found it "unmilitary and unsatisfactory.") Nevertheless, the Committee thought she would look good on television, and the committee controls the invitation list.

There were also investigators from the Government Accounting Office (whose investigation found nothing Defense hadn't already discovered), as well as the Small Business Administration (which had many other disagreements with Defense, and could be expected to be virulently anti-Defense), and even a former procurement legal specialist from academia.

Prepare For The Play

The Defense witnesses took the time necessary to thoroughly prepare. They reviewed the files. They personally and extensively interviewed key Defense people. They made pre-hearing calls on the Committee. They made other Congressional calls to ensure the issue was kept isolated to only one or two Committees, as well as to only one branch of Congress. They had coffee with the other Government witnesses. Displays were produced and edited for visual effect. Murder boards were held. Through careful review of the written statements, and with assistance from the White House, they prevented the Small Business Administration representative from placing unfounded (and false) statements in the Record.

The political appointees also decided that delegating the Buy American Act waiver authority to career civil servants or military officers was not only unfair to those individuals, but also a sore point for some in the Congress. A waiver is viewed as a political act by a segment of Congress. Given that, then logically a waiver decision should be made by a political appointee, who was expected to be more sensitive to, as well as answerable for, political issues. Defense announced a new policy on waivers before the hearing. This change was tactically effective, in addition to being the right thing to do.

During over four hours of hearings, some of the Congressional Members were emotional as well as personally abusive. Nevertheless, the Defense witnesses kept solidly on message: the Chief had made a decision that was his to make; procurement officials had properly waived the Buy American Act; and the beret procurement was professionally and properly done. They made their sound bites. They were respectful to the Congressmen, but steadfastly refuted any accusation of impropriety. After the hearing, the Administration witnesses carefully debriefed the Press.

The hearing was a draw.

<u>Which is the best you should hope for, when one side controls the microphones, the cameras, the questions, and sits on an elevated podium. A tie in an adversarial hearing is much better than kissing your sister.</u>

The Press wrote it up as a non-event.

But there was still a problem. The Army was going to get its berets, and the Chief's credibility was intact, but two Committees were still angry with the Department. In pique, would they continue to snipe at Army transformation? How could the issue be put to bed?

A few months later, the proper opportunity walked through the door. Remember the only American company that could produce berets? It was a small business in one of our poorer states, and the largest employer in their town. One day this small business "noticed" they had perjured themselves by certifying that all of the content in their berets was American-made. Almost all of it was American, just a little bit was made overseas. They asked, "Could we have a quick waiver to the Buy American Act, or will we have to stop production and throw a hundred people out of work?"

One could have thought of this as a setback. Without those

American-made berets, the Army had no chance of being in berets by its birthday! However, was it also a propitious opportunity? A couple of calls were made to the Hill:

- The Small Business Committee Chairman was notified there was a problem with the only small business in America making berets. Defense was evaluating what perjury sanctions would be necessary. Throughout the conversation, the elephant in the room was politely left grazing unnoticed — was the Small Business Committee going to be responsible for putting American small business employees on the street?

- The Congressman who represented the company's hometown, who sat on the Small Business Committee, was also informed of the problem. He was told that, in the light of current Congressional sentiment, Defense would only consider a waiver if both the Government Reform Committee and the Small Business Committee urged so, in writing.

A few days later, an appropriate letter arrived at Defense. This skirmish was over. Congress had agreed to a truce. Army transformation would continue.

Soldiers look impressive in berets.

Leadership and Management Rules

1. When there is controversy, find out all the facts before you take a position. Your credibility is your best personal armor. Subsequent retractions and corrections make you look weak.
2. Career civil servants normally do the best they can. When their performance justifies it, they should be aggressively protected. Their future professional performance will reflect their gratitude.
3. The facts of an issue, and the good work of thousands of men and women, can be undone though inadequate performance by a political appointee at a Congressional hearing. Don't fumble the ball inside the red zone!
4. Particular to the Pentagon, but applicable everywhere — a united front of Military and Political officials can be more effective than the best NFL "front four.

Chapter Eleven

THE PRESS

The faint of heart may wish to skip this chapter. There is no easier way to irritate your boss, his boss, and on up to the President, than to make an error dealing with the press. Many political appointees make an early decision to treat press members and hot stoves alike. That is definitely one way of operating. Avoidance may well be a lower risk path, but it does mean there will be missed opportunities.

To Talk or Not to Talk

There are two problems with the "hot stove" approach. One is that, no matter what your level of seniority, inevitably you are going to be publicly representing the Administration for some reason, and the press is going to ask questions and quote you, if only to get an attribution for the story. Will you be prepared, or will an incautious *bon mot* roll off your tongue and onto a front page?

Before going any further, let me reiterate that Public Affairs has an excellent media training session available. Each political appointee should participate as soon as possible.

The second downside is that you miss the opportunity to "educate" rotations of the press corps. For training and experience, news organizations move their people to different jobs. As a result, many of the men and women who write about your Department for important publications and media outlets start out knowing much less than they should about the myriad of Departmental subjects and issues.

Nevertheless, in spite of being on a steep learning curve, a newly-assigned reporter still has to turn out stories; it is his or her job. A reporter is going to be careful. No one in the press wants to be wrong – they have their peers and critics too — so they do diligence research. But if you avoid the press all the time, where are they to go to for information or a quote? Right, to the critics and active opponents of the Administration's position! Concurrently, the press' need for information is not always going to be always solved by your press relations office. Competent as the latter may be, they often can only handle headline issues before their time and expertise are overtaxed.

I believe that dealing with the press is like making speeches. The more you prepare and handle routine requests, the more likely you will be capable of a homerun when your team needs a round-tripper. But, in the meantime, be careful to always run out the singles. Your team looks very askance at an "out."

When talking to the press, use the same rules as when talking to Congress. Know your stuff and stay on message. *If you don't know the difference between "off-the-record," "background" and "for attribution," talk to your public affairs people.*

There is also a bureaucratic rule – know your boss. I once worked with someone who each week counted the lines publicly attributed to her, and then compared this total with the number of published quotes by any subordinates. She had a mysterious, hard to cure, disease common to the swampy areas located close to Foggy Bottom – *bureaucratic-big- head*. I worked for several others who I suspected of being exposed to the same affliction. They, at least, were subtle enough to count and compare subconsciously. Nevertheless, if you want the sun to continue to come up over your Washington home, take care not to outshine your boss with the press.

A less obvious problem with having your name in the papers too frequently is that, unless you are the Secretary or Deputy Secretary, the press may well think you are trying to manipulate them for self-aggrandizement, and treat you accordingly.

Stay On Message

Let's assume that you are going to make yourself available to Public Affairs to talk to the press. There are going to be three general situations in which you will find yourself:
1. The routine scheduled interview;
2. The press conference; and
3. The telephone call.

The first is the routine one-on-one, or one-on-few, interview with a reporter who is working a specific subject. The reporter will approach public affairs, which sets these interviews up and then accompanies the reporter to your office to physically sit in and record the session if there later becomes a need to keep all parties honest as to what was said. Your role in the interview is to transmit the message the Administration wants delivered. Remember the basic rules – know the story you want to deliver, stay on message throughout, and don't wander afield.

Stick Tight To The Truth

There are several problems with straying from the straight and narrow. The moral one was explained to us by our parents. The community rule we learned from our friends and peers. But you are an adult now. You are a public official. Have the rules changed? No, not for me, and I suspect, not for you.

Telling the truth is always easiest. Morality aside, the overriding practical reason for sticking to the truth is you don't then have to remember everything you've said before. There are going to be a great number of your comments on some sort of record, and, in the changing world, they only will be consistent if they reflect the truth (sometimes, when you are not as perceptive as you wish you had been, the "truth" only as you knew it at the time).

I don't know how some people in the public eye appear to believe they can lie and hope to ever remember the tortuous record trail they have left. Stick to the truth or don't answer the question. This policy saves you from later wasting time trying to "elaborate" or obscure your footprints in the mud. You have too much positive to do.

Stay in Your Own Lane

With the basic point of truth-telling emphasized, let's expand a bit on why you need to be vigilant to not "drift" during an interview. You may be an expert in many areas, but even if you make a living doing public speaking, most of us don't do our most articulate thinking on our feet. We can all benefit from a bit of time thinking about the clearest way in which an issue should be presented. Answering all of a reporter's questions, irregardless whether or not the query is relevant to his or her topic, is more than the reporter expects or deserves, and is inevitably an error.

So don't stray from the subject of the interview to address a peripheral issue. It may easily lead to bureaucratic quicksand. Even if you know a great deal about the issue at question, the answer may not be within your bailiwick! Don't let a reporter entice you into speaking on a subject on which you haven't prepared your thoughts. The unrelated issue may become the headline, rather than your carefully planned sound bite. Staying in your own lane will maximize the impact of your desired message, and minimize the number of apologetic phone calls you owe colleagues.

Now is a good point to insert a terribly important caution –

Classified Information. *You are going to read many papers and hear a lot of briefings. What is classified and what is not may well become smeared in your mind. You cannot make a mistake in this area. Why something is classified may not be apparent to you (particularly under the hot lights of an interview). If there is a* *possibility some information might be controlled, leave it compartmented in your mind, unconnected with your lips.*

End Runs. Often a reporter will try to go around the Public Affairs office and directly call your staff. This is a no-no. The professionals in Public Affairs know the reporters, know the publications, and have a good sense as to what the Secretary or President is comfortable with a subordinate discussing. Make sure your personal staff knows to politely, but automatically, refer all these requests down the hall to the proper office.

Press Conferences. The second situation in which you meet the press is the "press conference." Let's give this a little thought. If the conference is routine, it will be done by Public Affairs. If it is not routine, and is exceptionally good news (but not juicy enough for the President), the press conference is going to be held by the Secretary. What does that leave for you? Exactly — the non-routine, bad news, session!

A "bad news" press conference doesn't get scheduled unless there either is a problem or the Department has not managed to establish a credible position on that issue with the public. Neither situation is good. The only positive aspect of this assignment is that your boss has enough confidence in you to put you on the spot.

The task is going to be similar to a testimony before Congress, except you are going to have fewer potential allies in the press room. You will need to prepare, compose a statement to hand out, focus on staying on message, and literally exude credibility. Preparation and facts are going to be your best shield against the slings and arrows headed your way. If you don't have the facts on your side, buy a new suit and get a haircut so at least you will look good in the pictures.

Leaks. The last press interaction is the one that has much more potential personal downside than the "bad news" press conference. These are the phone calls from reporters wanting information. If you take these calls (for the record, note that I advise against it), the potential upside of talking to a reporter is that you can try to make him or her better understand the issues involved (of course, from the Administration's point of view, which is what the cynical sometimes refer to as "spin"). By listening, you also have the opportunity to discover holes in your knowledge or where "the story" you are advocating needs some shoring. The downside is the reporter often really wants to confirm or find out what was decided, or who said, during an internal meeting in the Department, the White House Situation Room, etc.

You can't tell the Press. There are many reasons, but lets just list a few:

Reason #1. It may be illegal. There are strict laws which apply to the proper disclosure of information, especially if you are dealing with classified information and briefings. There are also statutes about Congressional notification, in addition to informal (but equally important) rules regarding the timing and disclosure of political information, both to friends and opponents. In addition there are very often big financial and policy issues at stake. In discussions of what equipment to buy, legislation to seek or regulations to change, large sums of money may be hanging on alternative outcomes.

Reason #2. It is bad government. If your team can not have an internal discussion without the content leaking to the Press, the Team can't function effectively. Running the Government is complex. Press leaks frequently preclude some team members from adding timely value to the process. We have an open society. Once the Secretary or President makes an announcement, the Congress and the American people have the rest of eternity to question and (re)work a decision. Privacy of discussion before the public unveiling helps makes sure the plan doesn't sink before it is launched.

Reason #3. It would break an implied confidence. Many discussions take place within the Department in which an individual articulates a view only in order to move the discussion along or to plumb the reactions of those present. *That particular view may be politically incorrect, and may, in fact, not even be the individual's true position.* Nothing positive is ever served by those comments being reported. To minimize any temptation, I personally never took notes in a meeting as to who said what or even what was said.

Reason #4. You may be very wrong. Even though you sat there throughout the meeting at issue, and even participated, you may well not know what else is going on within the Government related to the meeting, or you may have missed some key body language from the principal. You may not have been invited to a critical follow-up meeting. I cannot even count how many times a reporter has called me with specifics about a meeting I had attended, with details that could only have come from an attendee, yet the conclusion/decision the reporter had been told **was absolutely wrong**. *(So what do I recommend in this event? Remember, the reporter may well be making the story up to get your reaction. I always said something like, "I can not tell you what went on, but what you relate doesn't sound like what I heard," and left it at that. If he is a good reporter, that note of caution will send him back to the drawing board. If he isn't, then his subsequent error will hasten his departure from this particular career path.)*

Reason #5. You have the potential to screw up the Administration's plan. A role out of an initiative is a complicated operation. Premature conversations with reporters have great potential to throw grit in these carefully polished wheels. A couple of words on this public unveiling, or "roll out," are useful for those who haven't previously served in the White House or at the top of a Department/Agency. Many bright minds contribute to the plan to make sure an important, and probably potentially controversial, decision is properly presented to the Congress, the American people, and the World.

Nearly everything is taken into consideration. First of all, the choice of the day of the roll out is important (what happened in history on that day, when do the weekly periodicals get put to bed?). The time is important (how does it conform to the news cycle, what is the difference in time zones in the countries who will be most interested, what is their news cycle?) The location is important (where is the President/Vice President/Secretary going to be if he wants to comment – is it the "right" forum for him to get a question? Who in Congress or elsewhere needs to be called and what is the message? Is there a different twist for different factions?) Who specifically is going to make each call? Etc, etc, etc...

Despite all the good reasons you should not leak information to the press, any reporter worth his or her salt is going to badger the hell out of you, and use all the tricks of the trade ("You mean you're not on the inside?") to get information. But you cannot blab and still remain a trusted member of the Team.

Leadership Rules

1. Make discussions with the press a deliberate decision. Stay on message and provide a sound bite. Help the press get it "right."
2. Stay in your lane in all public discussions. No matter how large your responsibilities, unless you are the President, your authority is limited. Don't tacitly intervene elsewhere
3. Press conferences require the same focus on preparation as does Congressional testimony.
4. Always tell the truth.
5. Don't leak.

Chapter Twelve

HEARINGS AND TESTIMONY

Congressional hearings are an integral part of any political appointee's trade. Hearings are an important forum for making the Administration's or Department's case. They are also your opportunity to prove you can think on your seat. In many cases, your fitness for more senior political appointments will be established at the witness table, in front of the men and women the American people have chosen to represent them in Congress. There is always the danger of a question you have not expected, and it is only preparation that will carry you over that hurdle. The most dreaded words I have heard on the Hill are, "If the witness is not prepared …."

Preparation

You can never organize too much for a hearing. Prepare, no matter if you are sitting second chair to the principal, or only are one-among-many from whom a Committee wants to hear. Prepare, even if the Chairman, or the staff, have promised a "friendly" hearing

— almost all hearings, no matter how advertised, are essentially adversarial. Someone in Congress is not happy about something, and wants answers. No one intends to look bad before the cameras and the press… at least, not on the Committee side of the table. Which, by the process of elimination, leaves only… you?

The keys to preparation are:

- know your subject;
- know your Congressional and Committee Members and staffers;
- practice; and
- stay on message.

First, you have to know your subject. This may seem obvious, but sometime you are going to be tasked to testify on a subject you knew <u>nothing</u> about only a few days before the hearing! Unfortunately, prior ignorance is not an excuse in this game. A Committee which can't be ignored has made a request and you have been adjudged of the right seniority and capability to absorb criticism, deflect disapproval, or make the Department's case. In other words, you drew the short straw. By the way, it may be on live television, so people around the world are going to judge both the case and you.

Of course you are too busy to prepare. Nevertheless, take the time. A two-hour hearing frequently requires at least twenty or more hours of preparation. It is terribly costly to your schedule and other responsibilities. But you must prepare. Rearrange your schedule as soon as you are tasked.

The first preparation step is to have your staff pull information together. Start your own reading even before the full briefing package is ready. The full package will have the questions your staff expects, along with recommended answers, but it may show up later than you need. While the staff is chasing down all the inputs, quickly evaluate the issue yourself. What is Congress asking? Is their question the real issue? What are the peripheral concerns?

When you get the package from your staff, read it quickly to determine what aspects of the issue you don't fully understand. Which answers do you find too good to be true? Who might have the information you need? Task your staff to find out. If you still aren't comfortable, make some telephone calls yourself and invite experts in for coffee.

What do you intend to say in your opening statement? An opening statement is written for every hearing, and must be cleared through the White House and all of the other Departments and Agencies in time to provide copies to the Committee at least 48 hours in advance. Someone on your staff has to get busy now composing that text. The statement is important and we will return to this subject.

Murder Boards

Personally, I like to have at least two "murder boards," or practice sessions, before a hearing. The first one should be several days before the hearing. Your Congressional Relations staff is going to take the lead in this board and ask questions they expect the Committee to pose. Other participants will chime in and offer follow-up questions, just as it will happen during the hearing.

I have watched more than one political appointee who was obviously uncomfortable being asked pointed questions by his bureaucratic juniors, and demonstrated it during the board by responding with humorous asides and rambling discourses. That is stupid. You may be senior in the murder board room, but you are going to be junior in the hearing room.

Treat the murder board as if it's the real thing. Use each board to purposely stress yourself. Keep it formal. Make this tough on yourself. It is the only way to prepare. When you reply to mock questions, make your answer exactly what you intend to say to the Committee. When you say something inappropriate, force yourself to work your way out. Discover the blind canyons of your logic in the privacy of the board, not during the hearing.

Encourage advice and criticism after the board is concluded. Ask everyone present for comments. They have given up their time to help you, and frequently from the mouths of babes .....
Consider each of their observations carefully. You won't take all

of everyone's advice, but many of these people know the Committee and the other players; so when they are listening to your answers, watching your body language and listening to your tone, they are also evaluating how those players will respond to your performance.

Then retire and lick your wounds in private. If you are too discouraged, ask your personal staff how you did. They will always praise you, no matter what the facts. However, they may subsequently ask to not sit directly behind you at the hearing.

The reason I always scheduled two boards was so that I could reflect upon the lessons learned from the first board, alter my approach accordingly and then have another opportunity to determine if a different approach was effective in delivering my message. Scheduling a timely board also made me focus and prepare early. If I were happy with my first performance, I could always cancel the second board. The designated board participants were always happy to get a couple of hours of their own back.

Other Witnesses

Frequently the Committee will ask other individuals to sit at the hearing table with you. This is always a subject of negotiation between your Congressional Relations staff and the Committee, but let's assume you are going to have company. The other witnesses, if they are from Government Agencies, are there because the Committee hopes to expose differences within the Administration. If the other witnesses are from the Government Accounting Office or the Inspector General's office, they are there to provide testimony critical of your Department, and from the Committee's perspective, to ensure the press gets enough meat for a good story.

So, why be blindsided? Why help the Committee make their case? Call up the other witnesses and invite them for coffee. When you meet, give them advance copies of your statement and ask for advance copies of theirs. They may well have good points or not fully understand the Department's intent. Often no one in the Department has ever paid them the courtesy of attention, solicited their views or discussed their recommendations.

Although it is last minute damage control, I have frequently defused a potential credible opponent's testimony by agreeing to some corrective action as late as a few days before a hearing. Even when I couldn't completely disarm the opposing testimony, the tone of the statement, or the witness's oral responses to Committee questions, became much more reasonable just because I had earlier listened. It is easy to dislike a stranger. One cup of coffee can change that relationship.

Preparation should also extend to the prime movers for this hearing — the Committee and their staffers. Extend them the courtesy of offering to discuss the issue before the hearing. You are gathering intelligence, and so are they. However, sometimes a preliminary meeting exposes their real issue, which may be substantially different from the one stated in the letter establishing the hearing. I have heard of hearings being cancelled as a result of a preliminary meeting. This may, however, be another one of Grimm's tales, for it never happened to me. If you can't schedule a meeting, get your Congressional Relations people busy earning their salaries.

Statement

A statement is a complex piece of paper. At first blush, a written answer to the Committee's written question may seem pretty simple and straightforward. But I am reminded that someone once described the written statement for a hearing as simply war by other means.

For starters, it gives you and your staff an opportunity to put the logic of your position on paper and look at it in the cold of black and white. The written statement also gives you the opportunity to make a record on complicated facts and history that you may never be able to get into oral testimony (or even recall completely accurately). The Members (or at least their staffers) will read it carefully and it will be part of history that is the Congressional Record

But take care, your statement may also open up lines of query that the Committee has not previously considered.

Since a written statement is cleared by the White House and the other Departments, it also can be used as a vehicle for arguing a case within the Administration. It may force another Department or the National Security Council staff to address issues which they may have heretofore steadfastly refused to consider until Congress scheduled a hearing. In this event, you are probably going to eventually have to revise your statement to remove the controversial sections before it goes to the Hill. However, you can use your initial statement to prevent the Department's position from being compromised by someone else in the Administration, who, without White House knowledge or approval for, may be promoting conflicting or opposing positions on the Hill. It is a big bureaucracy. Don't let someone use the Hill, and you, to end run your own Secretary.

Testimony

On the day of the event, get over to the Hill early and meet the Committee Chairman. Exchange pleasantries. Be pleasant. Even though some on the Committee may think you are the devil incarnate, you and they are all interested in good government. There is no sense in unnecessarily offending anyone, particularly now. If the sledding gets tough, you can benefit from any evenhandedness the Chairman might choose to offer during the hearing.

Put your key staffer in the seat right behind you. He/she will be in the line of vision of the Committee members and the camera. Her job is to stay awake and look like she agrees with everything you say, even while she is scribbling a note to pass you on some obscure fact (an obscure fact is an important one you didn't recall) or a bonehead thing you just said, which you will want to correct later during the hearing. She is your credibility backdrop. She must understand she can't frown or even twitch an ear as you are answering a question.

I do not like anything on the table with me but my oral statement and a pad of blank paper. Some witnesses take voluminous briefing books, but I have found their use as fruitless as using the text during an open book philosophy test. You should be thinking about what the Member is saying, watching the staff whisper in their ears, and thinking about your next answer, not flipping futilely through a thick briefing book. Besides, you don't need a manuscript, you prepared. Leave the books to your staff. One of their roles is to magically produce and hand you any document which becomes relevant.

After the chairman makes an opening statement, take a sip of water, politely lie about how much you appreciate being there and summarize your statement. Emphasize the message and the sound bites you have prepared. Ask that the statement be included in the record. Do not waste the Committee's time reading it.

Which is a good time to emphasize another aspect of hearings. This is the Committee's hearing room. If the hearing is being televised or the press is present (the latter will always be there unless the hearing is closed), it is an opportunity for the Members to get face time with their constituents. Nearly all members will have statements they wish to make for the record, and their own message and sound bites. Then the serious questioning begins.

One note — you run a very dangerous course if you decide to prove one or more Members wrong in public. If there are real errors of fact, this should have been resolved in a preliminary meeting.

You take the same risks if you lose your temper, raise your voice or are not otherwise unfailingly polite, no matter how wrong or foolish a particular Member's position. You may need that Member or his Chairman in the future. Besides, the issue may be a constituent one, and all Members get some slack on constituent issues.

There are a few other cautions. Never, ever, interrupt a question from a Senator or a Representative. You will get your chance. At the same time, do not allow yourself (and the Administration's position) to be browbeaten. You are both testifying and selling.

Never answer a question where you are unsure of the answer

(unknown Administrative policy, facts of some sort, etc.). It is always much preferable to take the question for the record and let the whole Department subsequently help you get it right rather than venture an answer that simply provides raw meat for the numerous ex-prosecuting attorneys sitting in the Committee. Overuse of this tactic will hurt your credibility, but weak or incorrect oral answers are even worse.

You can do it. Keep your cool. Stay on message. Use your sound bites.

When the hearing is finally over, stay on message while exchanging pleasantries with the Chairman, other Members and staff. The hearing is not over. The cameras may still be rolling. The Press is still there. In fact, if you or your staff don't talk to press representatives afterward, how can you be sure the reporters understood your message and got your sound bites?

Leadership Rules

1. Take whatever time is necessary to prepare for every hearing.
2. Contact the other government witnesses and appropriate Committee Members and staff well before the hearing. This may be where your earlier calls on the key staff members and your assiduous routine efforts to keep in touch will bear fruit.
3. Practice by using a murder board, and practice as you will play, treating the rehearsals as seriously as you will the hearing.
4. Pay as much attention to your statement as you would anything else which is going to appear in the Congressional Record with your name attached.
5. Stay on message during the hearing. Keep your cool. No matter what happens, your Mother will think you did fine. Deliver your sound bites.
6. Make sure the Press understands (gets your slant on) what took place.

Chapter Thirteen

THE INDUSTRY

As a political appointee, you make the regulations and policies that affect millions of Americans. This means there is an "Industry" that is dramatically affected by policies, rulings and regulations the Department/Agency establishes. Even before you are sworn, you may well be familiar with your particular industry and its interests. If so, you probably understand there are times they can assist the Department and Administration — as well as occasions when you are going to want to keep their representatives no closer than the longest pole you can find in your office.

So what is this "Industry" and how do you deal with it? One segment is composed of those people who make things — big things, such as loans, and houses, and roads and cars, or smaller items like popsicles and dolls, as well as the companies who focus on providing services — like doing income taxes and maintaining SouthWest's aircraft.

Still another industry segment is composed of the people who have made an industry out of thinking about the Government or the Department. Some are in "think tanks" directly employed by

Administration officials. Some are professors in Universities. Others, the "shadow-government" individuals, many of whom may have served in previous Administrations, now write, talk and lobby about issues from their own, and the party-out-of-power's, perspectives. These people deal with ideas – new or recycled — about organizing, operating, or just doing things differently. They are bright, experienced, people, and, if nothing else, they frequently expand your horizon about possible alternative solution sets. I recommend listening, or attending their conferences, as often as you have time.

No matter what your post, you are going to interact with representatives of your "Industry." They all will want to influence the way in which you think about issues affecting them, as well as how you use the money and authority Congress allocates. The generic term for this is lobbying. Lobbying is a fact of life for political appointees. Do not resent this process (it will be impossible to ignore), because it can bring you ideas you haven't considered, as well as illuminate aspects of an issue you may not have adequately weighed.

This being said in general, there is a very special industry which is going to be of interest to nearly everyone in an Administration and needs some special elaboration. I am referring to the industry which sells to Defense. To give you some perspective on the scale of business opportunities with the Department of Defense, about half of our tax dollars (not already earmarked for legally fixed requirements such as social security) go to the Defense industry. This industry is the dozen or more firms that focus on developing and manufacturing airplanes and ships and guns for Defense, the hundreds of small manufacturers who make a single product (military hats, earplugs), and the thousands of companies who provide services – providing Marines their meals and cutting Army grass.

The defense industry is not just the province of Defense. If you are in Justice, you are not only in charge of all legal action with these companies, but also the approval authority for all mergers, as well as the proposed acquisition of any US defense company by a non-American entity. State and Commerce will have a significant amount of interaction with the industry over issues of export and import control, as will the National Security Council and the Office of Management and Budget in the White House. Energy is going to find much of the defense industry is also its industry. Small Business is going to be interested in where the majority of tax dollars are spent, etc., etc. In addition, the industry employs a great number of Americans.

Nearly everyone in an Administration is going to find itself involved in this particular industry. Accordingly, a little background may be useful.

Innovation And Competition

There is a constant press, by both intellectuals and government officials, to find ways in which the commercial industry in America can meet Defense's needs. This makes great economic sense, as the United States' commercial industry today pumps much more money into technology research and development than the government could ever afford. Because of this investment, the large markets, and the impact of capitalistic competition, innovation flows from American commercial companies like water from an inexhaustible spring. If the military can use an "off-the-shelf" commercial product, it will be much less expensive (and probably more capable) than any comparable product made exclusively for the military.

This works wonderfully in some Defense areas, and not at all in others. For example, nearly everyone in Defense contributes to Bill Gates' growing wealth by using Microsoft. But Microsoft doesn't write software which can be used to discriminate between birds, sunspots and incoming missiles, nor can the software that makes your computer work guide a missile to intercept the right target.

At the same time, commercial companies have found it infeasible to balance the philosophy of entrepreneurship in the private sector with the regimen of controls which America demands over the spending of its tax dollars. As a result, commercial companies simply do not make military weapons. General Motors doesn't build Army trucks. Citicorp doesn't finance Defense acquisitions.

Why is this? Well, first is the issue of profit. While successful public companies frequently make thirty or more percent profit on their capital investments, the Congress and the Public look askance at such numbers in Defense. Defense contracts are written to reflect those Congressional and public concerns. As a result, the dividing line for profit in Defense companies is the low double-digit area. The better businesses make ten to twelve percent profit annually, and the ones on the low side of the average line make nine percent or less. Commercial companies can not afford to invest money for this rate of return.

There is also the problem of entrepreneurial flexibility. In a company making commercial products, a relatively junior executive makes many independent and unfettered decisions about what (and from whom) he will buy to put into his product. He is held accountable by his boss through the quarterly bottom line. If he pays too much or buys inferior goods, and can't subsequently make adequate profit, he will be replaced. If he succeeds, he will commonly be awarded bonuses of forty percent or more of his annual salary. If he is very good, or very lucky, he may be a millionaire before he is thirty.

There is no similar bottom line judgment in Defense. In addition, no matter how talented the Pentagon individual, we look askance at military officers and career civil servants becoming millionaires with our tax money.

The Defense industry is essentially a fettered industry. Congress nearly exclusively uses this industry to make social policy and to change the effects of historical inequities. As an example, Defense is strongly encouraged to spend half their dollars in buying from small businesses, at least a certain percentage purchasing from socially and economically disadvantaged businesses, another percentage buying from women-owned businesses, severely handicapped businesses, Indian-owned, etc. Defense is also required to openly compete every contract, from pencils and sink stoppers, to stealth airplanes. Alternatively, when I was in commercial industry, responsible for a program, I could call an individual whom I knew to be reliable and agree on a price and delivery details for a part over the telephone.

In Defense, such behavior is illegal. Defense is required to encourage competition between all of those who might be able to produce. Thus, there are a great number of records required, kept by both the manufacturer and the government, to ensure Defense is spending in strict accordance with all Congress directives. Many estimate these records alone add at least 20% to the cost of a product. It is an Industry cost of doing business in the manner that Congress (and by extrapolation, the American people) desires.

For these, and a variety of other reasons, Administrations have had difficulty in making Defense operate completely in accordance with an American commercial business model. At the same time, and not for the lack of trying (Defense executives understand the difference between 30% and 10% profits), no large Defense company has ever been successful in developing a large commercial business. (I except the jet engine business, where Pratt and Whitney, General Electric and Boeing provide the engines for both commercial and military airplanes. This is the one remaining area in American industry where the military research and development investment still drives technology, thus feeding both the military and civilian applications).

This situation is not a matter of good executives in commercial companies and poor executives in Defense companies. No large commercial company has developed a large defense position (Unless they simply bought a Defense business and subsequently operated it autonomously within the company – e.g., Boeing.) On the other hand, there is a long history of commercial firms making unsuccessful forays into defense work with the consequences of severely damaged bottom lines.

So, while Defense is currently saving money (and improving readiness) each year by deciding more and more tasks can be done by commercial companies (also known as "privatization"), the Department has found it impossible to find a substitute for those Defense companies which make purely military products (guns, missiles, submarines, attack airplanes, etc.). On the flip side, Industry companies have only one buyer — Defense.

This is a codependency, for America is largely dependent on competition within the Industry for innovation, as well as for the affordable products which are the touchstone of our military power. As a result, all Administrations are, whether they want to be, or not, involved with ensuring the Defense industry remains viable, as well as constantly worrying whether or not there is sufficient competition within the Industry to drive innovation and price control.

Change Agent

Despite these various constraints, the Defense Industry is all America has. The question for many Administration officials is how you use that industry to make change (the current buzz word is "transformation") feasible, as new uses of technology and new concepts are essential to continued American military and world strength. Political appointees have an important role in that process.

The way we practice capitalism in America helps to counteract the bureaucratic resistance to change. The Defense industry has a great number of people focused on one specific problem – it may be relations with India, it may be how to bend a metal part in one precise way. Through that focus, aided by the measuring stick of their own bottom lines, industry is constantly generating new ideas. Concurrently, companies are always trying to grow their particular business, whether it is ideas or processors, and to do so they have to either develop a new market or demonstrate they have a better idea/product than the existing one you are using.

How does this help America? Let us take a recent example. In late 2000, Defense selected Lockheed Martin to build the next manned attack airplane – the Joint Strike Fighter. This airplane is expected to be the only piloted airplane the United States will build for thirty years. With that decision, without further action, Boeing no longer has a future in manned fighter and attack aircraft. So, what naturally happens?

Several options are open, but the most likely is that in order to recover a market position in this important part of the Aerospace business, Boeing will focus on advocating unmanned aircraft to do the fighter/attack role. They will direct internal funds, plus do all they can to obtain Government funding, toward developing a Boeing unmanned fighter/attack airplane.

Now there have been several influential people (e.g., Senator Warner from Virginia) who have been discussing the advisability of unmanned aircraft for some time, but the majority of the military is generally most comfortable with what they know best, and during normal times, no major contractor will deliberately irritate its customer. As long as the military is buying Boeing attack/fighter airplanes, it is not in Boeing's interest to bite the hand that signs the checks. Remember that *99% of the money Defense spends comes through the Services and Agencies. Service civil servants and military officers have long memories about companies seen as undermining a particular service program or forcing the Service to go down a path the Service views as risky.*

However, if the customer has decided to go with a competitor in an important market segment, then all bets are off. If Boeing proceeds as expected, the American military will benefit from the resulting competition of ideas. Lockheed will be pressing for the new *status quo* (the F-35/ Joint Strike Fighter) and Boeing and other large defense contractors will be lobbying for faster development of unmanned alternatives. Both will come forward with new ideas, which Defense, and their political appointees, will then have to evaluate. Conceiving an idea is the hard part. Evaluating is much easier.

Dreaming up new alternatives is a great value of every Department's Industry.

Undue Influence

Each Agency is responsible for allocating or regulating the flow of a great deal of money, and there is not one in ten thousand Americans who understand either the checks and balances in the acquisition and contracting system, or how difficult it sometimes is to choose between two competitors.

As an appointee, you must do your part to enforce the rules and demonstrate that undue influence does not exist. The best way to show this is with your most valuable commodity – your time. It is very easy to fall into a habit of spending all your time with the major players.

However, if you are only attentive to the major players, you are not sending the right messages. It is particularly easy for a small business or organization to feel discriminated against since they lack the corporate funds to establish large Washington offices with staff to make contact with, or to carry special pleadings to, Members of Congress and Department Officials. Take the time to talk to and listen to all of the people who make America great. Do your part to make sure the Department behaves evenhandedly, and make sure the public knows it.

Defamation

Be very careful what you say in public, to the press or Wall Street analysts about a particular company – large or small. One reason is obvious: many companies are traded on a stock exchange. Traders and analysts have no idea that your comments probably have absolutely no relationship as to whether or not a company is going to be awarded a particular contract or be otherwise affected. Since they don't understand the inner workings of contracting, your positive or negative comments may well unduly and falsely affect that company's stock, creating opportunities for someone to make or lose money.

There is also another effect in play. I once listened to an official say something very critical about a company and its leadership. The official was especially frustrated, because he had been dealing for weeks with high profile problems that seemed all to emanate from that one company. That offhand comment, when inadvertently leaked to the Press, devastated the company's employees, who were actually doing very well in many other areas/

programs. In fact, the employees and executives subsequently believed the entire Administration was against them. As a result, they were reluctant to compete in areas in which competition is absolutely vital to American innovation. They gave up for a while –

At the same time, we were initiating a very important program in their area of expertise. We needed them to invest their money, their management and all their skills in developing new ideas and concepts. We needed them to believe they could win! I spent six months routinely giving pep talks to their employees to compensate for that one comment by another official.

Your Department's Industry is important. They are not only part of the fabric of America, but also an important source of our world presence. It is relatively easy to deal with them if you remember that their jobs and ideas are at stake. They therefore want to be listened to, taken seriously, and given honest and realistic feedback.

Leadership Rules

1. Competition produces innovation and controls prices. Continued innovation is important to America's ability to carry out our responsibilities in the world. The Government would not have the Department or Agency you serve in if it were not for the Government interests represented, in part, by the associated Industry and the need for a balance with the public good.
2. The Department of Defense needs the Defense Industry. The Defense Industry has no other customer. Therefore, political appointees need to worry about the health and competitiveness of the Defense Industry.
3. Because of the natural competition for both concepts and dollars, Industry is often the source of the majority of ideas that produce innovation and efficiency – take time to listen.
4. "Undue influence" is the cry of those who do not have access. Devote effort to dispelling this issue.

Chapter Fourteen

A Case Study –
Export Control

Most challenges in an Administration only involve one Agency. Normal problems that reach a political appointee's attention are never simple, and require you to think, consult, coordinate and establish a position within your Department/Agency, obtain White House concurrence from the National Security Council and/or Office of Management and Budget; and then sell the solution to "your" Committees in Congress. Each success is justifiably considered a significant accomplishment in an Administration.

However, every now and then you get to experience the full spectrum of working in a democracy. This occurs when you run up against an issue which involves multiple Agencies, each with their own culture, priorities and equities. If more than one Department is involved, the matter obviously has the interest of a large part of the White House staff, as well as many in Congress. These are special opportunities. The military sardonically terms such tests – "character builders." This is a case study of such an event.

Points to remember include:

* The Administration's political appointees are a team. You need to personally know as many of them as possible. There will be issues when you need everyone's help.
* For tough issues, you need the support of all the elements in your Department. To make each work together effectively, you need to understand their motivations and limitations.

Problem

During the Eighties, a spy informed the United States that more than 5000 Soviet weapons systems depended on American parts for their proper operation. To handicap the Soviets as much as possible, the United States instituted a strict policy which built on and expanded 1949 legislation by restricting the export of anything remotely considered "military." This program was very effective during the Cold War. Our Allies shared their technology with us and, in return, the United States provided the bulk of the nuclear deterrent for all of the free world.

After the Berlin Wall fell, the world changed. There was no longer a common threat to unify the non-communist nations. Thus, there was no longer an impetus for other nations to observe this one-way "military" technology street. Concurrently, the United States found it still needed Allies in order to support American interests – whether in the Gulf, Kosovo, Timor or Afghanistan. The American military was talking about interoperability and allied operations. However, the American export control system was preventing the transfer of technology which might enable such interoperability or facilitate successful allied operations.

The British reorganized their entire military so that it was fully compatible with their United States compatriots; however US export restrictions prevented them from effectively modernizing except by buying American equipment – at the expense of Brit jobs.

As you might expect, the British reevaluated this situation relative to their own national interests. With the Cold War over, they and our other traditional allies began making decisions that clearly demonstrated that our export control system carried an excessive political penalty for them. From their perspective, if the US export system weren't changed, interoperability would have to be sacrificed. In a short time, this foreign "boycott" began to spread to other American products, products with no obvious Defense applications, but still technically falling under the onerous and dated export control system.

As is often true, historical events often bring general trends clearly into focus. In this case, it was the military operations in Kosovo. Whatever the overall successes of the engagement, the interoperability weaknesses with our Allies were crystal clear. What would have happened if the enemy had been stronger?

The Defense Secretary directed that we bring the export control system into conformance with the Cold War era. His staff decided to do a little consultation. The Defense Industry and our career civil servants told us that the State Department was clearly at fault.

We called our State counterparts. They said that the same Industry, and their civil servants, told them that Defense was at fault. Since State, Defense and Commerce all have roles in the export approval process, we called Commerce. Their response:

"You both are impossible for either industry or other nations to deal with!"

Meanwhile State had apparently been thinking it over and called back, pointing out that Defense was part of the export control process (true); was doing just as bad a job in administering the system as State was (we had no idea if it were true or not); that Congress had given the President the task to establish such a system, and he had passed it on to State (true); that the Congress was very interested (true); and that Justice, as the enforcement agency, needed to be consulted (true). State further opined that State, Congress and Justice saw no need for any changes (true, but we hadn't explained our concerns to the Congress or Justice yet). State also opined that Commerce was not to be trusted (they seemed like nice folks to us).

We did some self-investigation. We also hired some outside

auditors, because using foxes to perform a chicken coop security review is often sketchy. When the facts were in, we discovered that our Defense system was so administratively complex and archaic that it was impossible to determine if the export system required by Congress could ever work in the post-Cold War world. One thing was clear. The system certainly wasn't working effectively now. We decided to reform our system, establish metrics of success, and institute every good management technique we knew. We would clean up at home before we looked askance at what were possibly weeds in our neighbor's (State) yard.

Within three months we could see internal improvement, and, within a year, the Defense system was ten times as efficient as before. However, the whole system remained bollixed, for State had failed to make any changes. They were continuing to talk, but not managing, and definitely not leading. We had run into a bureaucratic blockade.

Solution

The Secretary of Defense decided to sign a Memorandum of Understanding with his counterpart, the British Minister of Defence, which outlined a determination to work together more efficiently on military issues (including export control of military items).

The Secretary of State's staff was apoplectic. They pointed out that State was responsible for all negotiations between nations.

Defense said no negotiations were involved; "just two countries' military departments declaring a common interest in fixing some purely military issues."

State said, "No, this is clearly a backdoor attack on the export control system, for which we are responsible."

Defense replied, "How could you ever think that? We don't care if you continue to be obstinate about a policy which is completely destroying the trade relations with all our Allies and weakening our Country militarily and economically. That is your perogative."

Defense continued, "We are just trying to save our military relationships."

Then we added, "By the way, the Secretary is going to sign a similar agreement with the Minister of Defence of Australia next month."

The Secretary's action did raise the visibility of the issue somewhat.

The good thing was that most of the Administration's political appointees had been informally discussing the issues for almost a year. The appropriate people at Defense, State, Commerce and the National Security Council had become personal friends, even if our Agencies had different equities at stake.

We had also used a focused, but collegial, process to directly involve the military, the State Department careerists, and the appropriate career civil servants in the issue. After a year of discussion and fact finding, nearly all of Defense was solidly supportive of the need to revise the export control system. (In a large bureaucracy, you can never get everyone herded up and headed west; you just do the best you can.)

In Defense, we had made the good decision to clean our own house first, and to invite the other members of the Administration to observe and comment on our corrective actions to our house. In the process, we gave lots of speeches on the subject, but were careful not to ever criticize other Agencies to the Press. As a result, Defense had convinced many in the other Departments of our earnestness. They recognized we believed there was a problem and were willing to work hard to fix the parts for which we were responsible.

People are human. Honest sincerity impresses. Restraint is viewed appreciatively. Our obvious sincerity and year long restraint proved invaluable in ameliorating emotions when we finally began picketing the maligners' homes.

The Press was of great assistance in getting the story out. They were, of course, most interested in reporting disagreements within the Administration. But the Administration Team agreed on a message which emphasized the issues under discussion and never acknowledged the obvious fact that different players had different pages in their songbooks. The Press knew who was where, but since no official would go on the record, reporters spent most of the time explaining the issues and the alternatives to their readers, which was helpful.

Deciding to reform export control also required talking to our Allies and convincing them that change was in their own national security interest. They were paying attention, as you are when neighbors down the block start tearing down their porch and building something new. Not surprisingly, this overseas discussion and confidence building is at least as complicated as it is in the United States. This international discussion also takes longer because you don't have all the personal contacts and relationships which proximity and years of working together have given you within the American community of Government. We started early, and were still late.

At the same time we were doing all these positive things, we also made several mistakes. Most importantly, we failed to recognize everyone who might have "standing" on the issue. I failed to include Justice (the enforcement Agency for export control) and Customs (responsible for the border checks of exports) in our year of twice-weekly collegial discussions. It was an oversight.

When State finally agreed with a plan of action, it subsequently cost us an additional six months to then bring Justice and Customs on board. Neither of the latter was ever as fully a part of the Administration team as they would have been if we had but included them earlier.

We also failed to adequately involve Congress. This guaranteed opposition. The omission was simply an oversight, because we had gone so far as to reach out to important members of the other political party – those individuals who might have our jobs if the next election went to their Presidential nominee. The bipartisan support later proved helpful, but nevertheless, we failed to include Congress early enough for their staffers to be part of and monitor our progress, to be impressed by our arguments, and also have sufficient time to reconsider old thoughts.

Each of these errors was a mistake which made ultimate success much, much harder. Each misstep cost valuable time, which in turn made it more unlikely that we would succeed before a new Administration, with new priorities, was in office.

Surprisingly, the Defense Industry was not the help we had expected. If we were successful in revising the export control system, they were obvious beneficiaries. We were thus puzzled by their lonely position on the sidelines. We decided to do some interviews with the Chairmen of the large defense companies. They all went about like this:

(us) "Why aren't you doing anything to help?"

(them) "Well, we agree, as Americans, that the current export control system hurts the Country and also my company, but there are career civil servants at State and Justice as well as staffers in the Congress, who are not in favor of change. If you political appointees don't carry the day, those people will still be around when the Administration changes and they will remain in charge of processing any export request we make in the future.

"They are vindictive people. I can't take the chance they will hold up one of our (export license) requests while letting one of our competitor's slide through. I'm with you, but don't quote me.

"I hope you win."

Well, shareholder responsibility and all that — you couldn't fault their understanding of Washington.

After two years of discussion between State, Commerce, Justice and Defense, when the President ultimately decided what he wanted to do, the Team stayed on message. There were no "victory" press releases or interviews, so there were no **public** winners or losers within the Administration. This made it much easier for all the Team to continue to pull in harness.

State began negotiations to build on the Secretary of Defense's previous Memorandum of Understanding, and several other important changes were made in the export control process. When a new Administration was sworn in, the process of export control reform was still inexorably moving forward. Will it succeed? The jury is still out. Change is very difficult in Government.

Leadership Rules

1. Success may require intimate knowledge of the entire Government and the whole Administrative Team. Do your best to learn Washington and to spend the required time to know all your Team members.
2. Get everyone with standing involved in problem solving. On all issues, it is helpful, but on big issues, you absolutely must have each facet of the Department — the political appointees, the careerists and the career civil servants — pulling together. This is best accomplished by prior consultation. If they are all part of the process, they will eventually normally become allies.
3. Prior involvement of all stakeholders is a win-win practice. Those omitted from prior consultations will often act in a role of opposition — you have not given them the opportunity to become allies. If you give them the chance, and they still choose to oppose, their hostility will frequently be ameliorated because they better understand your concerns.

Chapter Fifteen
_____

THE MILITARY

You may meet military officers in various liaison jobs in Washington. As a consequence, it is useful for the political appointee to have a working knowledge of the career military officer. In Defense, this understanding is essential. The Military is where the rubber of Defense meets the road. If you become a Defense political appointee, you are going to work with a large number of military officers. You will find you frequently need their support in order for you to succeed. How do you best make this symbiotic relationship work? What are the problems you will have?

Conservative, Liberal or Apolitical?

We need to first discuss their politics. Military officers have a reputation for being very conservative. Democratic Administrations sometimes approach the military warily, as if they were Republicans in sheep's uniforms. Republican Administrations sometimes start out by assuming the military are brothers, or at least distant cousins, under the skin. Are either correct?

No. The military is apolitical, both by law and practice. Because this particular issue often unduly shades the early relations an Administration has with the Military, this is an important point to fully understand. It is the essence of each Service culture that duty in Washington, in the political arena, is **never** preferred to duty in the field or at sea. Each senior officer has been reared to believe this. The military does not like politics.

As we will later discuss, a few individual military officers may become very good in the Foggy Bottom milieu, but, as a whole, the political process is seen by the uniformed military as nothing in which a "good" officer would willingly become involved. A tour in DC may be one of the items on an officer's checklist to reach General, but it is not to be enjoyed. Verify this for yourself. Ask any senior military officer you meet whether he or she would rather be in the field, separated from their spouse and family, or in Washington? You will be surprised at the answer. Military officers are apolitical by inclination, training and choice.

On the other hand, all military promotion lists have to be approved by the Senate, which forces an intersection of the military and political worlds. Each officer promoted to three and four stars must be <u>individually confirmed by the Senate for each job he is assigned.</u> By the time an individual is Chief of his Service; he may have appeared before members of the Armed Services Committee a half-dozen times and testified to the Committee several other times. A relationship exists, as does respect, or the senior officer would not have continued to be confirmed.

That relationship can be helpful to the Administration when the military and political teams are in agreement, and is a factor that must be accounted for if they are not.

Just because the military is apolitical, doesn't mean that individual service members don't have a philosophical bent. Military officers appear more conservative that America as a whole for several good reasons. To begin with, it is very difficult for a senior officer to live in the U.S. military environment and not be operationally "conservative." From the time of General Grant during the Civil War, the US has held a hand in which, if the military didn't make big mistakes, the power of the US economy, generating ever more guns, ships, airplanes and new fruits of technology, would eventually guarantee victory.

In addition, with the great number of very capable officers constantly flowing into the Services from our Academies and Universities, and the military policy of up or out, there is constant competition in the Services for promotion. It is a fact of life that, when evaluating officers for promotion or a valued assignment, if one officer has failed to take the necessary precautions for his people, or is "just unlucky," there are more than enough other officers whose records, or professional reputations, contain no such blot.

Those officers who are not promoted, being human, naturally believe it is due to no fault of their own, and frequently ascribe the missed advancement to the fact they were "willing to take chances." You will hear this. It is frequently a discussion theme in the Military's own professional journals.

However, after you get to know the senior military officers well, you will probably be much less convinced of their aversion to risk. The military is a meritocracy and those at the top are extremely well-qualified. No senior officer is stupid. They have proven themselves professionally in a very demanding career field.

However, as we previously discussed, they have also worked within the same system for a long time, and, this frequently means they have not personally had extensive opportunities to see how different concepts might work. In this respect, military officers are, as a group, conservative.

It would also be a serious omission to forget Vietnam. All contemporary senior officers served during Vietnam or worked for those who did. No matter what the rights and wrongs were in this conflict, there is ample record that many of the groups who tend to be identified with Democrats supported those protesters who scorned the children, ridiculed the wives, and threw blood on the uniforms of military officers who were following the orders of the Commander in Chief.

That memory lingers and is still discussed around literal and figurative campfires. I suspect most military officers vote Republican in the privacy of the election booth.

Nevertheless, individual senior officers may be quite liberal in view. I well remember during the Nixon Presidency when the Chief of Naval Operations, Admiral Elmo Zumwalt, personally decided the war in Vietnam was lost, turned it over to a Captain to run, and devoted his own efforts to equal rights and respect for Hispanics, Blacks and Women in the Navy.

One afternoon, as Admiral Zumwalt finished a live press conference to announce that he was putting women on Navy ships, the press corps spotted the Republican Secretary of the Navy departing his own office down the hall. Seeing a photo opportunity with both the Chief and the Secretary on the same day, they surged toward the Secretary.

Lights again lit up the Pentagon's E Ring corridor, cameras began rolling, and a reporter stepped forward and placed a microphone in the Republican Secretary's face, "Mr. Secretary, what do you think about women on ships?" the reporter asked.

"Not in my Navy!" the Secretary averred. Perhaps there was a difference in political views. The two individuals later ran against each other for Senator.

Parochialism

The point of this story is that the Chiefs of the Services believe they have a sacred duty to both preserve and improve their Services. This Chief of Naval Operations had decided that the Navy would be unable to recruit sufficient high quality people in the future unless he included women and eliminated racism in the Navy. It may also have been an issue of right or wrong, but to him it was a matter of the survival of the Navy. He had decided to dedicate the power of his Office to that end, rather than worry about what he felt was an unwinnable war. He had not discussed his priorities with the President. He had definitely not discussed putting women on ships with the proper appointed officials, neither the Secretary of the Navy nor the Secretary of Defense. He was going to do what he thought best for the Navy. (It is a matter of history that the Secretary of the Navy later won the Senatorial campaign.)

I have known many, many senior officers who were innovative and acted equally independently from both the conventions of their peers and the history of their service.

However, the focus on preserving and improving the service whose uniform they wear is both the strength and the weakness of the military officer. This poses a dilemma for military officers serving assignments in the Joint Staff organization. The Joint Staff, the Chairman's staff, is made up of representatives of all branches of the Services, Active, Guard and Reserve. Even when an officer is wearing his Joint Staff hat, it may be difficult for many to make a decision which, while possibly in the best interests of Defense, or the Country, might appear detrimental to his own Service.

In addition to his Service bonding at birth, the "system" encourages service loyalty. There is no "Joint" assignment or promotion staff. The Services influence all promotions. A military officer is not only promoted by a board of his uniformed peers, he is also assigned, or recommended for assignment, even for the most senior jobs, by the chief of his service. That frequently serves as an unconscious deterrent to an Army officer, even if he knew enough about the Marine Corps to believe it, from publicly endorsing using a (Marine) Expeditionary Battalion, rather than the (Army) 82nd Airborne, for a very visible assignment.

The good political appointee can help senior military officers overcome those subconscious obstacles.

Systemic Flaws

Let me quickly review an important point made previously. There are two basic (and un-American) structural problems in our American system of Government: lack of competition and the existence of centralized organization and control.

There is little competition within Defense, because maintaining competing defense systems is unaffordable. Correspondingly, there is no bottom line by which to judge decisions and there are no quarterly reports for analysts to pore over. Defense is a monopoly with all the inherent disadvantages of such. The Country gets some pseudo-competition by comparing the Army to the Marine Corps, and the Air Force to the air arm of the Navy, but actually holding either discussion is practically verboten in the Pentagon. Broaching the subject is considered akin to pouring gasoline on the fire of interservice rivalry.

Without direct competition Defense is missing the market forces that naturally direct, no matter how painful, the redistribution of capital from old technology industries (or warfighting concepts and systems) to new ones.

The second basic problem in Defense is that each Service is centrally organized, controlled and operated. This centrality of control is a great system for warfighting. Central control is very effective at putting coordinated force on specific objectives in the field. However, the same system may enable a few impressive, qualified, but shortsighted, officers at the top of a Service to stifle initiative, innovation and the proper application of capital to new breakthrough technologies.

For fiscal and warfighting reasons, Defense must live with these two potentially disastrous threats to America. Political appointees in Defense are essential to minimizing the ill effects of these structural flaws.

Experience Limitations

Although many military officers have traveled extensively and understand geopolitics much better than many of their civilian peers, the military officer also lives his life relatively removed from America. Military officers frequently live on bases, camps or stations, surrounded by fences, and they spend their working hours with a very elite stratum of our society.

At the same time, a military officer is very, very busy. Warfighting is a complicated and demanding art, which becomes even more challenging as the military drives to higher standards, uses more high technology systems, and focuses on dealing with diverse, world-wide, threats. Learning and practicing to be a warrior requires literally years of work and experience. It is the rare aspiring warrior (and the Services generally only promote warriors to their key billets) who has extra time to stay abreast of what is new in society, technology or business.

Symbiotic Relationships

With a little care, the military and the political can both help each other in an Administration. The political appointee knows what the President desires, and may well have a clearer picture of the cultural, business and technological changes afoot in the world. On the other hand, the senior military officer has worked for years to hone his skills in organizing troops, military operations and the effective application of force. This is the recipe for a very productive symbiotic relationship — you are both interested in doing a good job for America. As in any team endeavor, get to know the key military personnel and demonstrate your interest in improving Defense. The military, individually and collectively, will normally leap at the opportunity to cooperate.

What happens when you and the military disagree? While there may be a common goal, as we have discussed, there are also differences in personal experience which may lead to differences of opinion. What should you do then?

What you can not do is dictate a change without discussion. The Military belongs not only to the President and Secretary of Defense, but also to Congress and the American public. If you can't resolve important differences, then you are going to have to debate them on a public stage. It is usually worth however much time is required to try to resolve the issue, rather than to subsequently spend the extraordinary amount of time arguing in open debate (and the political administration may ultimately lose, remember the TFX in the sixties?).

The specific practice of resolution is easier to strategize if you understand that no Service is any more a monolith than are the Republicans and Democrats. Each Service has different factions, often centered on career specialties and experience, which may well feel completely differently about a subject. No matter how carefully and definitively one view has been labeled as "The Air Force Position," it is usually only one of several views held by factions in the Service. Using this knowledge is a political act and you are a political appointee, so I leave you to your labors.

If you can't settle differences an important military faction believes are important, then you will find that there are specific Members of Congress who pay particular attention to and protect specific Services. A senior military officer doesn't have to shift too uneasily in his witness chair to induce a Senator or Representative to "demand" the officer's personal opinion. The Defense Press also knows many senior officers, and their telephone numbers – perhaps better than yours! Don't be too surprised if, on occasion, you recognize a particular slant to a press leak.

You are only going to "control" this process by the power of your argument and the openness at which you arrive at decisions within the Pentagon. No matter how emotional the issue, if all the stakeholders come to believe they have had a fair opportunity to make their points, you are more than halfway toward success. It is slow, but it is the only way to get true change that will survive throughout the political process in Washington external to the Department.

Leadership Rules

1. Military officers are generally "conservative" in their views, but apolitical in their Party preferences.
2. The bulk of a military officer's experience has been in one of the Services, and he or she is much more familiar with the capabilities and culture of that Service.
3. The military officer has lived much of his life in a relatively closed environment, and thus, while very aware of the improvements within the militaries of the world, may be less cognizant of equally dramatic changes in societies, business and technology.
4. Because Defense is a monopoly and the Services are centrally organized and controlled, there are not natural and powerful forces within the military which drive change.
5. Military officers who strongly disagree with the Administration will be heard by Congress and the Public. At the same time, it is the rare issue that can not be resolved by prior consultation.

Chapter Sixteen

A CASE STUDY– GLOBAL HAWK

The American "system" of Government often relies on political appointees to make real change possible. The key leadership and management qualities in this case study are:

> *Unlike American business, Government has no "bottom line" to force change, however painful, in resource allocation. Political appointees must both drive and facilitate necessary change, lest your Agency become as weak and irrelevant as a subsidized buggy whip industry.*

> *Recognize which decisions are particularly difficult for your organization's "culture." Act accordingly.*

There are two possible "models," or ways in which to think about, our National Defense. One is to postulate a situation in which you are not sure of the possible forces which could be arrayed against America, nor where they might strike. In those countries which can afford it this condition drives an arms race in which (Cold War) one economy eventually subsumes, with or without direct enemy action, or (World War II) the enemy is eventually defeated after a costly struggle, or (Vietnam and Korean War) the enemy is contained.

A second model is one in which you have perfect knowledge of the enemy's intentions, and capabilities, and are able to defeat him by striking surgically at one or a few of his essential links. Despite its attractiveness, most of us believe the later concept is an impractical dream. Even given perfect knowledge of capabilities, one can never, with full confidence, know the intentions of those currently in power in countries which might seek do us harm, much less the intentions of those who might come to power in the future.

In fact, neither of these models is best for America. Our system is wisely constructed to have our Generals and Admirals trained and focused on both uncertainty and possible threats. They remember that, in less than five years, Germany rose to be a world threat in the '30's and the USSR did the same in the Fifties. Since they will have the responsibility for executing any war, Generals and Admirals are always going to be more comfortable with more, rather than "enough."

This brings us to the debate on "enough" versus "excessive," for excessive dollars spent now on Defense are dollars consequently not available to invest in American infrastructure and the development of new technologies. This means fewer dollars to fuel continued the American economic growth which has, in turn, enabled our strong Defense.

Since "excessive" is largely in the eye of the beholder, as is the current "threat" assessment, the President and the Congress annually struggle to balance this trade-off in the annual Budget process.

In this Budget debate, as well as in planning for and executing military missions, better knowledge of the enemy's capabilities, while it cannot do it all, helps fill in more of the capability/intentions matrix. However, some military personnel may be strangely ambivalent about better knowledge which leads to our ...

Problem

Unmanned military vehicles have been around for a long time. For years we have used drones as targets for anti-aircraft practice. Nearly three decades ago, we invented the Tomahawk missile, which is essentially a low altitude, long-range, unmanned, guided and preprogrammed weapon. The Tomahawk has been used as the initial strike weapon (to take out the key initial targets, or degrade the enemy's air defenses) in nearly every engagement since it became operational. In another venue, two decades ago Israel demonstrated the use of unmanned surveillance air platforms to support ground combat.

Unmanned military vehicles have some obvious advantages. It is well understood that the human support package in a military airplane takes up a great deal of weight and space, and that there are valuable military missions in which one may be loath to risk a human. However, since the first airplane went aloft in battle, the human pilot has provided an invaluable trained brain. With the advent of ever more capable computers and more complex software, along with the continuing miniaturization of processors, the technical question has been clear for years — when would the human pilot be a military disadvantage (the weight of his support system not worth his or her added value) in performing some military missions such as surveillance?

Despite the obviousness of the question, aggressive United States development of unmanned aerial vehicles has been an off and on activity. In 2000, the Air Force finally took delivery of the first unmanned platform which could go a long way, stay up a protracted time, and carry sufficient payload to perform several missions concurrently – the Global Hawk.

Why did it take so long?

Technology

Technology advances are never a smooth path. New technology develops by fits and starts. While an unusual person may be able to clearly see a bright future in a particular technological application, for complicated challenges like military platforms (military-speak for weapon delivery systems such as tanks, airplanes and ships), it is often many years before sufficient technology comes together to realize that vision. Early on, most of us can't tell if it is Paul Revere we hear or just another false alarm.

For example, nearly everyone believes that submarines are an important component of our Defense. But they have been a long time getting here. The Turtle engaged the HMS Eagle during the Revolutionary War. The next submarine was not bought by the United States until 1900, and it wasn't until 1954 that nuclear power made Nautilus the first true submersible.

Investment

If you don't invest, you don't get. When you have a military platform driven or piloted by individuals, many extraordinary military people are going to be attracted to the newest capability on the block (the thrill and personal danger involved in flying a combat airplane, a space shuttle or operating a tank). Later in their careers, they will identify with their younger days when they lived on the cutting edge, risking life and limb. On the other hand, the idea of an unmanned vehicle is not nearly as exciting. It certainly doesn't promise much adventure to the typical warrior.

Aerospace engineers may be interested in unmanned vehicles. But if exceptional military officers are not, the unmanned project is going to be near the rear of the line for extraordinary funding. The project is also not going to be the subject of journal articles written by uniformed leaders whose personal reputation and life stories inspire men to join the new venture.

Culture and Budgeting Problems

In all the Services, a new idea takes money from some established program. A new technology will thus always experience some tough sledding. This can be worse in some Services, if their budgets are built in a decentralized manner. For example, in the Air Force, Global Hawk was considered to be a surveillance platform. Therefore, if it were to be supported, the Major Commander responsible for surveillance had to take money from some other, probably already underfunded, program, in order to buy this new unmanned airplane. At the time of this case study, the appropriate Commander was struggling with an aging, increasingly expensive, U-2 program.

Now the U-2 program is the stuff of which legends are made. Books are written about it. Schoolchildren know its name. The inventor is famous. The company is famous. Some of the men who flew U-2's went on to become astronauts and Generals. The company who built the old ones was also more than willing to build replacement new U-2's to keep the tradition and this essential capability alive!

There is another, unvoiced, cultural problem. The Global Hawk could dwell precisely over a site, essentially hovering in the air around the clock while providing all-weather pictures, monitoring communications and doing other military tasks. In the parlance of the day, it could provide real-time, precise intelligence.

This was both a dramatic new development as well as a threat to business as usual. There have been satellites providing information for years, but, due to the laws of orbital dynamics, if the satellite is to "see" one spot continuously, then it has to be 90,000 miles up in the sky. This great distance limits what the satellite can "see" and "hear."

It you need better information, a satellite can be launched at a lower altitude of only several hundred miles, but now the satellite is whizzing around the world so fast (a physically necessity to stay aloft), it can't continuously watch one spot, no matter how important that area is at the moment. The U-2 airplane, while flying closer to the target than a satellite, has some of the same tactical limitations.

By contrast, Global Hawk could essentially <u>hover</u> at about 60,000 feet. It can remain close but not too close, out of the range of most dangers, giving the commander a continuous eagle's eye

view. It can be under the direct control of the local military commander, looking at what he wants, communicating directly with
him. Global Hawk has the promise to provide precise intelligence
for the tactical commander.

However, if you combine precise intelligence with precise
weapons, what happens? Well, of course you get greatly enhanced
military capability, but what else? The force size in our Army,
Navy, Air Force and Marine Corps is based on achieving over-
whelming force. Do we need as many of those forces if knowledge from an unmanned vehicle increases the probability of hit-
ting the right target by a thousand percent or more?

Are you still going to need the same number of airplanes and
ships and tanks? Are we going to need the same size Services?
(There are very good reasons we will still need large numbers of
different forces, but that is another discussion. The point is that
the expansive use of Global-Hawk-type-vehicles might well add
credibility to those (generally anti-military critics) who are always
proposing a smaller military.) Even thinking about reducing the
force structure, or the number of people in the Services, is always
a very emotional issue for the military.

Global Hawk presented cultural, as well as technological, problems to the military.

Solution

After several years of floundering in all the Services' unmanned
aerial vehicle programs, the Secretary of Defense did the following:

He removed all the unmanned programs from the Services'
oversight until after they were developed. The aerial vehicles were
assigned to a special program office which reported directly to an
Under Secretary for Defense. Concurrently, several new programs
were also started to explore the limits of the technology.

*(Interestingly, the two programs which succeeded, Global Hawk
and Predator, were both ones developed by small companies considered fringe members of the defense industry. Was it because the*

small companies did not have other large contracts with the Serv-ices, who had failed to embrace unmanned aerial vehicles? Was it because the small companies were truly more innovative? I don't know.)

The Department Secretary (actually three Secretaries in a row provided personal leadership on this issue) paid unrelenting inter-est to the development of the unmanned aerial vehicle program. As part of the Secretariat's special attention, they insisted on pro-viding separate and adequate funding for the unmanned vehicle programs, despite the Services' continued disinterest. Through arm-twisting, they kept the Service lack of interest from developing into active opposition.

Even after Global Hawk proved effective during test flights, the Military Services and Major Commands still ignored it. US military interest was finally piqued, when, after successfully test-ing in the Pacific, the Australians expressed interest in buying sev-eral.

Meanwhile, the appropriate military and civilian officials in the Air Force and Navy were encouraged by the Defense Secre-tary to publicly support the Global Hawk program. The Secretary of Defense has a great number of tools to encourage good behavior. He used them all. The Air Force was finally won over by not only giving the Air Force extra funds which could be used only for the development of Global Hawk, but also permitting them to use mili-tary personnel to control the flight of, and maintain, the aerial ve-hicles. (Many believe both functions were more expensive and less effectively performed with military personnel, but why should the Secretary simultaneously take on another large dragon?)

When the next conflict occurred, Global Hawk was deployed to the war zone, even though it was not yet certified as "opera-tional" by the Air Force. The capability got rave reviews from the commanders in the field.

Nearly a decade after the Secretary of Defense had personally taken over development of unmanned aerial vehicles, the Chief of Staff of the Air Force and the Chief of Naval Operations both an-nounced plans to buy Global Hawks, and they wanted them now!

The President announced major Defense budget increases to buy "precision weapons, unmanned aircraft..."

The Military had finally, firmly, stepped onto the path of unmanned aerial vehicles.

Leadership Rules

1. "Culture" is usually good, but sometimes it can prevent the entire organization from recognizing a breakthrough opportunity. Culture consists of more than uniforms.
2. Funds and time spent on obsolete answers delay developing new relevant solutions, but Government Agencies operate without the help of a bottom line in redirecting resources or policy. Established answers may continue to be funded or supported, even after they become technologically or socially archaic.
3. A solution imposed is frequently a solution opposed. There are compromises available which make innovation less painful, but innovation is never achieved without strong leadership.
4. No "disruptive" technology was ever introduced without exceptional leadership.

Chapter Seventeen

A CASE STUDY — ANTHRAX VACCINE

If you are very privileged, sometime during your political appointment you can bring all you have learned in Washington to bear on a truly important issue. This is one such case. It illustrates the following:

> *Doing the "right thing" is frequently neither popular nor easy. Not knowing the correct action is understandable. On the other hand, when you are fortunate enough to discover the proper path to the top of a mountain, giving up because the trail is rocky, overgrown or steep, is not forgivable.*
>
> *You have to be able to accept bad news with grace. Taking out your frustration on your subordinates loses your followers. Overreacting to setbacks disappoints your supporters. You must be able to compartmentalize your disappointment within, in order that you, your subordinates and supporters, can continue to think. As Kipling said so well,*

"If you can keep your head, while all about you are losing theirs, and blaming it on you....
Yours is the Earth and everything that's in it."
*Some fights in Washington are truly difficult — and not
everyone on "your" side will always want you to win. If you
are going to take on a fight, learn the facts first. Before you
proceed, conduct a final check to make sure the challenge is
truly worth winning. On the other hand, if the cause is just,
and remains so, never disengage. Never.*

A Lengthy But Necessary Background

During the Cold War, the arms race not only included a race in
nuclear weapons, but also a race to find mind-altering drugs, poi-
son gases and deadly diseases which could be "weaponized." What
exactly does that last term mean?

The active ingredients in dynamite can be readily "weaponized,"
which means that a chemical mixture can be melted, poured into a
metal shell, stored and transported safely and then fired from a
mortar, gun, or released from an airplane to produce a controlled
explosion. On the other hand, most gases, such as the phosgene
gas used in World War I, are difficult to effectively weaponize.
Since they are containerized under high pressure, they may leak
while being transported, which is not good for our side. Their delivery is also difficult, as gases don't readily disperse evenly over
large areas. Even when finally deployed in anger, while deadly in
the immediate vicinity, most gases soon lose their effectiveness as
they spread out.

Bacteria are another story, particularly the anthrax bacteria. The
anthrax spore occurs in nature and is very hardy. It can live for
years in the grass, through the hottest summers and coldest win-
ters, until it is inhaled by a grazing animal or human being. Once
the spores are in the lungs, the disease kills within a few days.
From the viewpoint of weaponry, anthrax can be weaponized by
using common crop dusters to spread the disease spores, and in
other ways that are still classified.

It is a matter of history that both sides worked at weaponizing anthrax during the Cold War, but the United States stopped this effort after signing the Biological Weapons Convention in 1972. As we suspected, and determined for sure after the fall of the Berlin Wall, the Soviet Union continued anthrax weaponizing experiments for a further twenty years.

After the dissolution of the Soviet Union, the United States learned that the Soviet Union had also helped construct anthrax manufacturing facilities in several other countries, generally countries (North Korea, Iraq, etc.), with whom the United States still had sharp and recurring disagreements. This was a real danger.

If our soldiers were unexpectedly attacked with anthrax, they would have to be immediately treated with antibiotics, evacuated and placed under hospital care. They could only remain in the field as an effective fighting force if their immune systems had been previously conditioned to resist the bacteria. After due deliberation, the Secretary of Defense, upon the request of the Chairman of the Joint Chiefs of Staff, made the decision to inoculate all military personnel serving near the countries of concern.

This program generated a public relations firestorm. It is worth explaining why.

The anthrax vaccine had been originally developed to protect individuals working in the cowhide and sheepskin garment industry. The vaccine was developed to react quickly (within 72 hours). The vaccine had to successfully energize the proper human defense mechanisms to fight and kill the disease before the patient died. This anthrax vaccine was (and remains) the only known total cure for anthrax. Special antibiotics can fight the infection from the bacteria, but only the vaccine kills the anthrax spores.

As with most inoculations, there are side effects from the vaccine. To begin with, it is the most painful shot I have ever taken. With each shot, I felt I could actually feel the stuff physically reorganizing my blood. If the internal effects were simply my imagination, the knot at the site of the shot was not. The knot lasted several days or weeks, always serving to remind me that I had injected something powerful in my body, and needed to do so again in a couple of weeks (it took six inoculations to guarantee immunity). This was tough medicine. If you were, for example, a Christian Scientist, and your religion counseled against shots, the (unharmful, but real) reaction might well heighten your natural apprehension.

If you were not fond of needles, the series of shots was a real downer. Of course, dying is also a depressant, and the troops in the field in the areas next to North Korea, Iraq and Iran, didn't object. They did not set about writing nasty letters to their Congressmen.

However, others did. The Secretary of Defense had directed everyone going into potentially hostile areas to be inoculated. This affected a large number of Active Duty, Guard and Reserve members who preferred, all in all, to take their chances. There were Reservists who only piloted cargo planes on weekends, as well as some Active Duty military personnel who were planning on ending their military service well before their units would ever rotate to a danger area. If your military unit were in Delaware or North Carolina, it was easy to be sanguine about the effects of anthrax on the other side of the Pacific. So, as you may remember from the press coverage at the time, a few individuals decided they didn't want the shots and, in some cases, were willing to be court-martialed rather than be protected against a "new" danger they couldn't see with their own eyes.

Another group of critics included some soldiers who had fought in the Gulf War and were dismayed that no cause for the Gulf War Syndrome had ever been established. Theory after theory had been proposed, examined, and then discarded. Several Americans were "sure" there was a Government cover-up. One of the possible "smoking guns" was the vaccinations (including anthrax) the men and women had been given in preparation for the build-up and subsequent Gulf War.

The anthrax inoculation program was a full bag of challenges – a new threat few understood, far-away places, religious inhibitions and the Gulf War Syndrome.

The Under Secretary of Defense for Personnel and Readiness devoted three years of his life to establish a national environment in which the Secretary's and Chairman's anthrax vaccine policy could be implemented. He did an extraordinary job. I will leave it to his memoirs, and those of his key assistants, to recount their success in finally obtaining military, Congressional and public acceptance of this new and controversial program.

However, there were two other significant aspects to the anthrax vaccine plan. . One was the ticking clock. How long until someone decided to use anthrax warfare against the United States? Many experts thought we were already living on borrowed time.

You also needed lots of vaccine if you were going to inoculate lots of people.

Problem

There were only two places in the Western World where the anthrax vaccine was made. One was a small facility in England, which was closed for renovation. The other was a larger, state-owned, public health facility in a Midwestern State. The latter made the only anthrax vaccine approved by the Federal Drug Administration (FDA) for use in the United States. The Midwestern facility also was temporarily closed for expansion. The public didn't realize it, but no one in the Western World was making the vaccine. Defense was living off existing, constantly shrinking, stocks.

Well before the Secretary of Defense had announced his intention to make anthrax inoculation mandatory, the Governor of the Midwestern State had decided his public facility was no longer an asset to his fellow citizens. He put the site up for auction. *I believe he also suspected that the facility was costing the State much more than was recorded on the books, and when a private company subsequently bought the facility, he was proven absolutely correct! The Midwestern State had been selling Defense the vaccine at about two dollars per dose. The real cost to the State to produce the vaccine turned out to have been in excess of $12 – clearly an unusual case of a State subsidizing the Federal Government!*

Several small companies bid to buy the company. None of the large drug companies bid. The anthrax vaccine was considered an "orphan" drug by the latter. Even if the vaccine were to be given to all two million military personnel, that market was still too small for a large company to make real money, especially considering the manufacturing dangers (part of the process requires working with live anthrax bacteria). In addition, as one drug executive explained to me, "We sell a lot of drugs overseas. We don't want to be seen as working with the United States Defense Department on drugs."

The company that bought the vaccine producer from the Midwestern State had never operated a vaccine company before. As it turned out, before they were able to produce the drug to FDA standards, they would spend nearly two years assembling an adequately experienced management team.

To correct problems previously identified at the Mid-Western facility by the FDA, as well as to expand the facility to meet the new, much, much, larger Defense requirements the new threat demanded, the old facility had been demolished and rebuilt. This led directly to an unforeseen problem.

Unknown to the company or Defense, the Federal Drug Administration had decided to significantly tighten and upgrade its requirements for approval for manufacturing vaccine products. The strictest and most time-consuming reviews would be for companies constructing new facilities. The FDA ruled that tearing down and rebuilding a facility on the same site was equivalent to building a new facility.

This was a major setback for manufacture of the anthrax vaccine. When we looked at the FDA/Drug industry history, it became obvious that the investigation process for an established company, with many other products and lots of money for consultants, could be expected to involve at least sixteen months. But this was a small company, and America only had enough vaccine left for eighteen months.

The clock was ticking. The supply of anthrax vaccine dwindled daily. Some problems in the vaccine facility were fixed, others were found. Tensions rose, fell and then rose again in Asia.

Tick. Tick. Tick.

A bureaucrat in the Pentagon insisted that the new company honor the old agreement the Midwestern State had signed and continue to sell the Defense Department the vaccine at a loss of more than ten dollars a dose. The company announced that if it did so, it had less than two months of operating capital and would have to go out of business. Some in the Pentagon and Congress decried the amount of money that was being devoted to vaccines against biological warfare. Others pointed out that the anthrax vaccine program could be funded for ten years for the cost of only one aircraft.

A team of experts advised the Defense Department that development of a new vaccine against anthrax would take a minimum of eight years.

This was clearly an unsatisfactory answer.

A second team was convened. They looked more carefully and estimated that, with unlimited funds, an FDA-approved vaccine could be produced in twelve to fifteen years. Ouch! The estimate was going the wrong way. Our only choice was to get the Midwestern facility up and operating.

The General responsible for the anthrax vaccine program recommended the company be permitted to fail. (He never could explain to me where we would then get any vaccine. Apparently he was very sensitive to the negative pressures from the Congress, his peers and the press.)

Tick. Tick. Tick.

Solution

The key was in recognizing that, while the Midwestern company had become privately owned, it was still the only company that produced a product America had to have. A Government take-over was evaluated as the worst possible solution, so the alternative was to treat the private factory as if it were a Government Facility (like hundreds of others in America). The existing contracts should be torn up and as much money invested as proved necessary, while, at the same time, putting Government auditors within the company to ensure the company owners and managers did not profit (and were paid nothing but their basic salaries) until they produced satisfactory vaccine.

But Government bureaucrats, whether wearing uniforms, or mufti, don't often think this way. Contract regulations are not written for this possibility. Military managers aren't taught how to manage such an arrangement. The situation languished. The company's own money would now run out in ten days. The company asked about loans. No banks or investors were interested in getting involved in this controversy.

The Company was still at least a year away from obtaining FDA approval.

More troops rotated to SouthWest Asia. More inoculations were given. It was discovered that our stockpile of vaccine was even smaller than thought. Iraqi soldiers were seen practicing flying crop dusters. Tick. Tick. Tock.

A senior political appointee took control of the manufacturing program. He established one rule. "There is a real threat. We must do everything Defense can do to help this company produce FDA-approved anthrax vaccine as soon as possible." He took the following action:

He replaced everyone who did not believe or follow this rule. He replaced the General running the program. Later, he replaced the replacement General.

He asked the company's Board of Directors to replace the President of the Company. They did. He insisted they scour the Country for better executives. They did.

The existing contracts were discarded. Government funds were provided the Company. Government auditors were assigned to audit every dollar spent and ensure no company executive received a raise or a bonus until vaccine was flowing to the military. On the other hand, milestone achievement bonuses were established for the blue-collar workers.

Everyone in Government who had expertise on anthrax or vaccines was asked or assigned to help the company.

The Company was defended in the Press.

The Company was defended in the Congress.

The Company's progress was critically reviewed weekly by the best team the Government could put together.

Each week, for at least a year, there was more bad news; more delays and more problems, with more money and more experts needed. Each week there were more pundits, in Congress and elsewhere, who recommended the program be terminated. "This is too hard. There really isn't a threat," they said.

Each month there were fewer political allies. "It isn't worth it, there is too much heat," they said.

Each week another press show or periodical took another critical shot at the anthrax program and the people running it.

Tick. Tock. Tock.

The new management team worked on. Individuals who faltered were replaced. The team worked through new problems. They invented new solutions. Months sped by. Anthrax vaccine stocks melted away. The chorus of boos grew even louder. Previous program supporters sought protective cover. Yet the political appointees in the Administration continued to protect the Company. A Member of Congress launched the latest in his attempts to kill the vaccine program by directing that a criminal investigation be conducted to determine if the political appointees were trying to save the company for their own personal gain.

11 September 2001. Terrorism on a scale not imagined, followed by anthrax attacks on Members of Congress and common citizens. Once the attack was recognized, antibiotics were used to help people fight off infection. Only a few tens of thousands of vaccine shots remaining in reserve — what if the attacks became widespread before the stores of vaccine were replenished?

10 January 2002. FDA approval of the Midwestern anthrax vaccine facility. The millions of doses manufactured in order to demonstrate the process were cleared and released to the Defense Department for stockpile and use. After a four year effort, we finally had enough vaccine to deal with a determined anthrax attack against the United States or her Allies.

Well done to all those in the Team who persevered!

Leadership Rule

"Never give in, never give in, never, never, never .... Never give in except to convictions of honor and good sense."

Sir Winston Churchill.
Address at Harrow School. October 29, 1941.

ISBN 155395172-7